"Can You Complete The Puzzle?"

(A Journey Towards Spiritual Growth and Direction)

VOLUME 2

Verdree B. Stanley

author**HOUSE**®

AuthorHouse™
1663 Liberty Drive
Bloomington, IN 47403
www.authorhouse.com
Phone: 1-800-839-8640

Published by AuthorHouse   05/22/2012

ISBN: 978-1-4772-1217-2 (sc)
ISBN: 978-1-4772-1218-9 (e)

Library of Congress Control Number: 2011906957

Any people depicted in stock imagery provided by Thinkstock are models, and such images are being used for illustrative purposes only.
Certain stock imagery © Thinkstock.

This book is printed on acid-free paper.

Because of the dynamic nature of the Internet, any web addresses or links contained in this book may have changed since publication and may no longer be valid. The views expressed in this work are solely those of the author and do not necessarily reflect the views of the publisher, and the publisher hereby disclaims any responsibility for them.

Preface

The Lord himself warned, "In the world you shall have tribulations" (John 16: 33). When attempts are made in understanding the Bible, it can become a puzzling experience. Learning what the Bible is all about in its truest form is a journey. Too often, the approach used to interpret the Bible consists in taking every phrase and every sentence as if that small portion of the text contained theological dogma in and of itself, and taking each saying as if it were to be understood in a literal manner. In such an approach, phrases and short sentences from the Scriptures are cited to support bias theories and ideas when these phrases and sentences do not carry the meaning imposed upon them. It is the task, therefore, of each person to make every effort to understand properly and critically the teachings of the various biblical materials. God wants us to choose to love him freely, even when that choice involves pain, because we are committed to him, not to our own good feelings and rewards. He wants us to cleave to him, even when we have every reason to deny him.

Table of Contents

Introduction

First, I must say, that I have only skimmed the surface in this 2nd volume of the word of God. The teaching of God's word is a life-long task. I have selected various chapters of each book of the Holy Bible. Each book of the Holy Bible has its own crossword puzzle, I have given each crossword puzzle much prayer, and spiritual guidance has come from God. After the group or individual, have completed all crossword puzzles in my book he/she will:

1. Acquire the ability to succeed in life with positive outcomes.

2. Become encouraged and not let negative behaviors take control over one's life.

3. Become Loyal to those around you and using those experiences for learning and understanding various situations.

4. Become mature by developing the necessary skills to distinguish levels of development.

5. Become confident by learning from past and present experiences.

6. Become free by thinking and meditating on spiritual matters.

7. Become Joyful in the mist of self doubt, having faith; All things are possible.

Tools Needed For Completing This Book:

- Holy Bible (King James Version).
- Pencil, Eraser, Note Pad.
- Biblical Concordance.
- Webster Dictionary
- All scriptures are from the Holy Bible.
- The answer to each puzzle is in each given scripture.
- On each puzzle grid, the answer can be; Across or Down.
- Definitions of terms are taken from; Biblical Commentaries, Biblical Dictionaries and Webster's Dictionaries.

Note;
   Working through each puzzle will bring blessings your way.

Genesis

Across:

2 - Which brother was sold into Egypt? ch; 45

3 - The first book of the law or Pentateuch,

6 - Jacob and Leah's daughter was named_____. ch; 34

7 - Esau and Jacobs's mother's name_____. ch; 25

11 - There are_____chapters in the book of Genesis.(kjv)

12 - Esau was older than his brother_____. ch; 27

15 - After Sarah died, Abraham married_____. ch; 25

16 - Sarai name was changed to_____. ch; 17

18 - God had promise Ismael he too, would have many_____. ch; 25

Down:

1 - Jacobs grandfather's name was_____. ch; 28

2 - Here comes this dreamer, he is a master at that._____ ch; 37

4 - Lot's wife looked back and became a column of_____. ch; 19

5 - Isaac mothers name is_____. ch; 17

6 - Joseph worked for an important man called_____. ch; 39

8 - The name Abram was changed to_____. ch; 17

9 - Lot's older daughter had a son who she called_____. ch; 19

10 - Pharaoh said to Joseph "P was standing on the land by the_____river" ch; 41

13 - Mesopotamia, its modern name is now_____.

14 - Lot was Abraham's_____. ch; 19

17 - There was a famine in_____. ch; 26

19 - God created the world in_____days. ch; 1,2,

Genesis

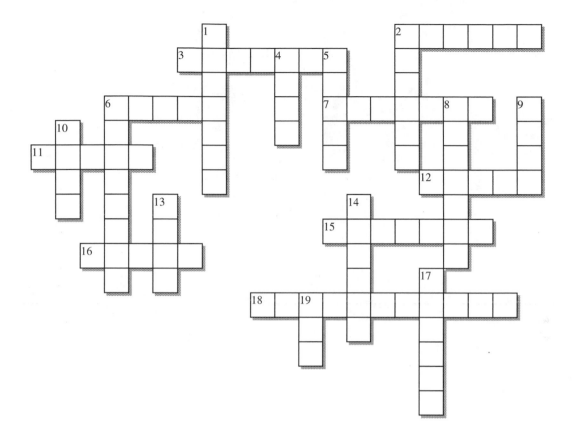

Notes

Exodus

Across:

2 - Sexual impurity. ch: 20

4 - I _____ you out. (This is what God does for us) ch: 20

5 - And Moses' anger was_____hot. ch: 32

7 - The disease was considered incurable. ch: 4

10 - And they shall cover the face of the earth. ch: 10

11 - Take thy rod and cast it before_____. ch: 4

12 - Stop. Take your_____off. ch: 2

13 - "_____ hand" generally associated with power. ch: 15

Down:

1 - The book of Exodus has_____chapters. (kjv)

2 - They are descendants of Esau's grandson. ch: 17

3 - He said to the Lord, "I am not_____" ch: 4

6 - This summary commandment helps us to remember the other nine. ch: 20

8 - A stone more valuable than diamonds. ch: 24

9 - Another name for Sinai. ch: 2

Exodus

Notes

Leviticus

Across:

1 - If a _____ sin. This is the first mention of sin offering required of the people. ch: 4

2 - _____ fire, in the sense of being foreign. ch: 10

4 - _____, he must have been saddened realizing the results of his indulgent attitude. ch: 10

6 - Two_____; offerings for abnormal conditions. ch: 15

9 - The Lord reserved a part, as He claims a portion of our time and of our income. ch: 2

12 - Do not_____. This is a clue that the use of alcohol was involved in the rebellion. ch: 10

13 - If a soul commit a trespass and sin through_____, ch: 5

Down:

1 - The wave_____Christ opened the way for our resurrection. ch: 23

2 - The voice of_____. This is a call for all witnesses for a trail. ch: 5

3 - The book of Leviticus has_____seven chapters. (kjv)

5 - "Whole_____" rather, the tail which had fat in it. ch: 3

7 - _____ bread. Yeast (leaven) represented sin. ch: 23

8 - Baken with_____. This symbolized the time when the Holy Spirit would be given to enable human agents to work with Christ. ch: 23

10 - All except a memorial portion. ch: 2

11 - Holy_____. They were times of corporate worship. ch: 23

Leviticus

Notes

Numbers

Across:

2 - By means of_____, God said that he had blessed Israel. ch: 22

6 - Balaam _____about a king who would come from Israel. ch: 24

8 - Reuben's tribe and Gad's tribe owned many cows and_____. ch: 32

9 - Balaam saw a_____from God. ch: 24

10 - The Israelites defeated the Amorites in the city called_____. ch: 21

13 - The priests used the trumpets for____reasons. ch: 10

14 - Balaam and Balak built_____alters. ch: 23

16 - _____ came from the tribes of midian. ch: 10

17 - The book of Numbers has_____six chapters. (kjv)

Down:

1 - _____ is from the Hebrew word "Nazir" It means to separate someone or something from everything else. ch: 6

3 - The smaller room was called the_____Holy place. ch: 1

4 - The bigger room was called the_____place. ch: 1

5 - _____ was the chief leader of Levi's tribe. ch: 3

6 - All of Aaron's sons' were_____. ch: 3

7 - Zubulun's tribe must camp on the other side of Judah's tribe. Their leader is_____. ch: 2

11 - God spoke to_____. ch: 1

12 - Balaam loved_____. ch: 22

15 - Judah's tribe must camp by the_____. ch: 2

Numbers

Notes

Deuteronomy

Across:

2 - Love and obey the_____. ch: 11

5 - A _____can be either money or things that a man leans to his neighbor. ch: 24

7 - _____must not mix with them by marriage and they must not pray to their gods. ch: 20

8 - The_____were the special servants of God. ch: 12

10 - God tells Moses what will_____to the Israelites. ch: 31

11 - The Israelites did not believe that God would_____for them. ch: 1

12 - The Israelites were_____. ch: 1

Down:

1 - _____ talks about the careful love of God during the forty years. ch: 8

3 - We were in the_____called "kedemoth" when I sent a message to Sihon. ch: 2

4 - The countries of Og and Bashan were not in_____. But the families of Reuben, Gad, and Manassah returned to live there. ch: 3

6 - The Israelites would not_____ God's word. ch: 1

9 - The_____of Moses. ch: 34

11 - The book of Deuteronomy has thirty_____chapters. (kjv)

Deuteronomy

Notes

Joshua

Across:

4 - God told the Israelites to walk around_____for seven days. ch: 6

5 - Joshua said to the Israelites, come here and listen to the words of the Lord your_____. ch: 3

7 - Joshua gave land to the tribe of Judah; and he divided it between the various_____. ch: 15

9 - Israel took their land. This land was_____of the Jordan. ch: 12

11 - Joshua and the Israelites made a_____with God. ch: 24

13 - Joshua spoke to all the people at_____. ch: 24

14 - The Israelites crossed the river of Jordan on_____ground. ch: 4

Down:

1 - Joshua was a man with_____. ch: 1

2 - The_____land was on the west side of Jordan. ch: 1

3 - The_____did not have any land of their own. ch: 21

6 - _____ trusted in the God of Israel. ch: 2

8 - So Rahab put a_____out of the window. ch: 2

10 - There are_____four chapters in the book of Joshua. (kjv)

12 - Joshua chose_____men. ch: 4

Joshua

Notes

Judges

Across:

4 - Samson loved a woman in the valley of Sorek whose name was_____. ch: 16

7 - And he divided the three_____men into three companies. ch: 7

9 - Barak was the son of_____. ch: 4

10 - _____vowed a vow unto the Lord. ch: 11

12 - And she caused him to shave off the_____locks of his head. ch: 16

13 - _____said unto her, if thou wilt go with me, then I will go. ch: 4

14 - Samson kills a_____. ch: 14

16 - She was a prophetess. her name was_____ ch: 4

Down:

1 - Then_____who is Gideon; ch: 7

2 - Samson poses a_____. ch: 14

3 - If I be_____, then my strength will go from me. ch: 16

5 - Samson demands a_____wife. ch: 14

6 - _____ was king of Canaan, that reigned in Hazar. ch: 4

8 - And the woman bare a son and called his name _____. ch: 13

11 - _____; or prostitute. ch: 11

15 - The book of Judges has twenty_____ chapters. (kjv)

Judges

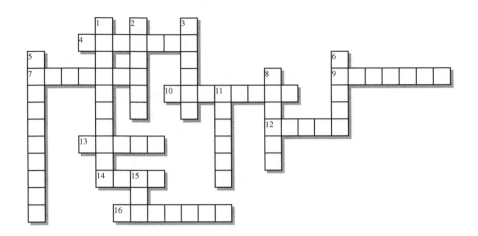

Notes

Ruth

Across:

4 - He turned and discovered a woman lying at his_____. ch: 3

5 - Ruth was_____than Naomi. ch: 2

6 - A type of grain. (see reference page)

7 - The baby's name was_____. ch: 4

9 - So Ruth went to the_____floor. ch: 3

12 - Amminadab was the father of_____. ch: 4

15 - Naomi had a_____. ch: 4

16 - Rachel and Leah help build up the house of_____. ch: 4

18 - Elimelech wife's name was_____. ch: 1

20 - Boaz said that he would take_____to be his wife. ch: 4

Down:

1 - Perez was the father of_____. ch: 4

2 - Naomi wanted what was best for them. She could not give them new_____. ch: 1

3 - _____and Ruth were from Moab. ch: 1

6 - The name "Mara" means_____. ch: 1

8 - Boaz kept Ruth's_____secret, so that nobody would think bad things about her. ch: 3

10 - Nahshon was the father of_____. ch: 4

11 - Time when food plants do not grow. (see reference page)

13 - She is better to you than_____sons. ch: 4

14 - Ruth fell on the ground to show that she_____Boaz. ch: 2

17 - _____ was a relative of Elimelech. ch: 2

19 - The book of Ruth has_____chapters. (kjv)

Ruth

Notes

First Samuel

Across:

4 - The philistines believed that their gods lived in the_____. ch: 4

6 - "Man of God" is another name for _____. ch: 2

8 - "The Rubbish Pile" is where people threw their_____. ch: 2

11 - It was more powerful than the other gods._____ ch: 5 (see reference section)

12 - _____ bread. Only the Priests were to eat this and only in a Holy place. ch: 21

14 - One of two stones in the breastplate of the high priest through which God commanded his will. ch; 28

15 - Hannah was desperate when she_____. ch: 1

16 - The Book of 1st Samuel has_____One chapters. (kjv)

18 - And poured it upon his head. It indicated prosperity. ch; 10

19 - Hannah wanted a_____so that she could give him back to God. ch; 1

20 - The_____of the covenant. ch: 3

Down:

1 - Every year Elkanah left Ramathaim and went to the town of_____. ch: 1

2 - A place just south of Jerusalem. ch: 21

3 - The woman's question implies that the Spirit had revealed Saul's hidden identity. ch: 28

5 - Hannah gave birth to a son, she called him_____. ch: 1

6 - Hannah prayed a prayer that was full of_____ to God. ch: 2

7 - "Oak of Tabor" "_____ of Tabor" old trees were good landmarks. ch; 10

9 - Elkanah had sex with his wife_____. ch: 1

10 - Elkanah Lived in the town of _____. ch: 1

13 - It is from the verb "naba" "to act as a spoke man for God. ch: 10

17 - The Philistines return the Ark of God to_____. ch: 5

First Samuel

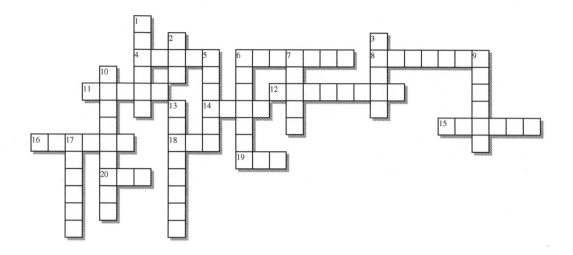

Notes

Second Samuel

Across:

2 - _____was expecting David's baby. ch: 11

4 - _____was wicked and he caused trouble. ch: 20

7 - Mephibosheth could not_____. ch: 9

8 - The Gibeonites put the men's_____on a hill. ch: 21

9 - _____becomes the king of Judah. ch; 2

13 - Abishai was Joab's _____. ch: 16

14 - The writer calls these men, ""The_____" ch: 23

15 - The men of Judah said, "we did this because the king is our close_____. ch: 19

17 - Lsh-bosheth was one of the son's of_____. ch: 2

18 - _____was David's wife. ch: 6

19 - Absalom had three sons and a daughter. His daughter's name was_____. ch: 14

22 - _____means perfect. Like something that is clean. ch: 22

23 - Then Nathan said to David, "You have behaved like that_____man" ch: 12

24 - Every country that David defeated had to pay_____to him. ch: 8

Down:

1 - David had six sons while he was in_____. ch: 3

3 - She gave Amnon_____reasons why he should not touch her. ch: 13

4 - David was not_____. ch: 7

5 - David builds an_____to the Lord. ch: 24

6 - The_____hired 20.000 Aramean soldiers. ch: 10

10 - Hushxi spoke to Zadok and Abiathar the_____. ch: 17

11 - One of David wives was named_____. ch: 2

12 - David was_____about his son Absalom. ch: 18

13 - Recab and_____killed Ish-bosheth ch: 4

16 - One of the names of the children David in Jerusalem was_____. ch: 5

20 - The Book of 2nd Samuel has Twenty_____chapters. (kjv)

21 - Davis went up to the hill called, the "Mount of_____" ch: 15

Second Samuel

Notes

First Kings

Across:

1 - Soloman reigned_____years. ch: 11

4 - Then Adonijah_____sheep, cows, and young fat cows. ch: 1

9 - From the top of Carmel, you can see the_____sea. ch: 18

10 - Elijah's_____was a special one. ch; 19

12 - Asa succeeded_____in the southern of Judah. ch: 15

14 - The sea was something special. It was full of water. The priests used this to wash themselves when they went into the_____. ch: 7

16 - God grants Jeroboam another chance by sending a_____to him with a warning and a sign. ch: 13

18 - _____, son of Soloman, succeeds to the throne. ch: 12

20 - _____is a stick with a sharp point. ch: 22

Down:

1 - A_____means, a time when people do not eat. ch: 21

2 - Maybe the_____was a road round, or on, the walls of Jerusalem. ch: 9

3 - It says, Soloman made. But it means that his_____did the work. ch: 6

4 - We_____when we do not obey God. ch: 8

5 - A_____is a large black bird. ch: 17

6 - The Hebrew word_____means "son" or "son of." So Ben-Hur is son of Hur, and so on. ch: 4

7 - _____means tell someone that they are good and great. ch: 5

8 - A_____is a big house that a king lives in. ch: 3

11 - There was an abnormal increase of_____. ch: 14

13 - _____is a material that people got from animals. ch: 10

14 - The book of 1st Kings has Twenty_____chapters. (kjv)

15 - David told Soloman that some people were dangerous. They included Adonijah, Abiathar, Jaob, and_____. ch: 2

17 - _____was a false god. ch: 16

19 - _____is another name for Syria. ch: 20

First Kings

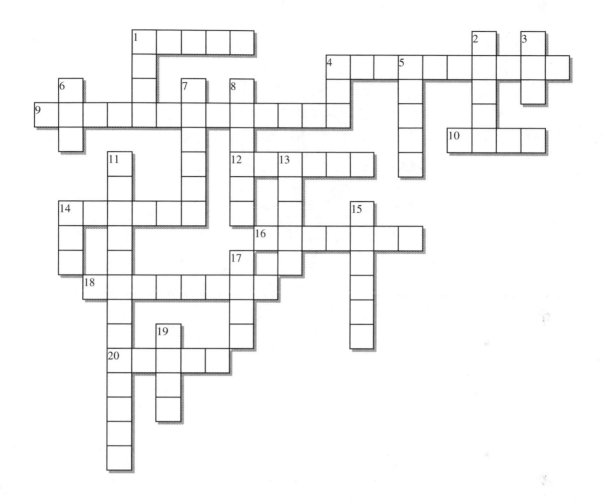

Notes

Second Kings

Across:

2 - The book of 2nd Kings has Twenty_____chapters. (kjv)

5 - "The King's House" was usually near the_____of the city. ch: 9

6 - _____an amount of money among the Jews. ch: 7

7 - _____was the king in Judah between 868 B.C. and 847 B. C. ch: 1

9 - The kings of_____caused their people to worship Baal. ch: 3

12 - The word for people, really means_____. This means a man's gift to his children when he dies. ch: 21

14 - The valley of_____is a valley south of the dead sea. ch: 14

15 - "These people" were the 70 sons of_____. ch: 10

17 - When the king heard the words from the Law_____, he tore his own clothes. ch: 22

19 - _____was the capital of Syria. ch: 16

20 - Athaliah was the_____of Ahaziah. ch: 11

22 - _____was the king of Babylon. ch: 24

24 - Naaman had an illness called_____. ch: 5

Down:

1 - A_____in Judah, means that a descendant of David would always rule in Judah. ch: 8

3 - _____was king for 17 years. ch: 13

4 - The word_____means, "a piece of bronze" but in Hebrew, it is the word for "snake" ch: 18

5 - _____was Elisha's servant. ch; 4

8 - "Little_____" is Nahar or Naar in Hebrew. ch: 2

10 - Merodach-Baladan was the king of_____. ch: 20

11 - One of the four descendants was_____. ch: 15

13 - The donkey's_____was used for food. ch: 6

16 - The priests_____that somebody else would make repairs to the house of the Lord. ch: 12

18 - They buried people outside the city in the_____valley. ch: 23

21 - Then they destroyed Zedekiah's_____. They tied him with a line of metal pieces that joined together. ch: 25

23 - People thought that their gods lived in their own_____. ch: 17

25 - Very hairy clothes: people wore_____when they were very sad. ch: 19

Second Kings

Notes

First Chronicles

Across:

2 - _____, a grandson of Hattush. ch: 3

3 - Chief_____, head of the 12 tribes. ch: 27

6 - _____, A natural result of following the ways of righteousness. ch: 22

8 - _____. Apparently for keeping the temple cups and other things clean. ch: 23

11 - He explained all in_____from the hand of Yahweh upon me. ch: 28

14 - The book of 1st Chronicles has Twenty_____ chapters. (kjv)

15 - Sent them_____. The wives were apparently sent away. ch: 8

18 - First_____, the religious year began in the spring, late March to late Aprilfor us. ch: 12

20 - _____. This was Mount Moriah where Abraham had prepared to sacrifice Isaac. ch: 21

24 - _____. A fortress overlooking the valley of Ajalon. ch: 14

25 - _____ the heart. He tests us to strengthen us. ch: 29

27 - The focus is on_____and his soldier sons who were slain. ch: 10

28 - _____. This gate may have been to the city land fill, where trash and filth was taken. ch: 26

Down:

1 - _____his brother in verse 10 has been popular. ch: 4

3 - Ram was Jerahmeel's_____son. ch: 2

4 - Abraham had sons from_____different women. ch: 1

5 - _____. The Hebrew word means, "Abode" or "Place to live" ch: 17

7 - Trees_____. Because the devastation of natural things must come to an end. ch: 16

9 - _____. He was the son of Zilpah. ch: 5

10 - _____, explaining the process. ch: 24

12 - _____, the one slain by the young David. ch: 20

13 - _____and Abiathar, the priests. Abiathar had escaped the slaughter or priests at Nob. ch: 15

16 - The lineage of_____is traced back to Gershon, son of Levi. ch: 6

17 - _____, or "set apart" or "consecrated" ch: 25

18 - _____, A town east of the Jordan in the tribe of Reuben. ch: 19

19 - _____, also known as, Kirjath-Jearim. ch: 13

21 - _____. It was replaced every sabbath. ch: 9

22 - Brought_____, or agreed to pay tribute. ch: 18

23 - _____, mighty, men; from this verse to the end of the chapter; These special men are described. ch: 11

26 - _____that is, men of military age. ch: 7

First Chronicles

Notes

Second Chronicles

Across:

2 - Solomon asked God to give him_____and knowledge. ch: 1

5 - King Asa removed his grandmother from her function as_____mother. ch: 15

6 - After the dedication of the temple, Solomon built his_____. It took him 13 years to complete it. ch: 7

8 - To make each_____object, Huram first made a model of it. ch: 4

11 - Amaziah would not_____to the advice of God and the prophets. ch: 25

13 - _____was 22 years old when he became king. ch: 33

14 - There was much_____in Jerusalem. ch: 30

16 - Asa and his army chased them all the way to the town called_____. ch: 14

18 - The prophet Isaiah made a_____of Uzziah's rule. ch: 26

19 - The prophet Isaiah son of Amoz, wrote about a_____. ch: 32

20 - The Levite musicians stood on the_____side of the alter. ch: 5

22 - The book of 2nd Chronicles has Thirty_____chapters. (lkv)

24 - Solomon told_____that Israel's God is greater than all other gods. ch: 2

Down:

1 - But_____sent men to Josiah. ch: 35

3 - King Solomon gave to the queen of_____all that she desired. ch: 9

4 - Rehoboam chose Abijah, son of_____to be the chief prince among his brothers. ch: 11

6 - Because of his evil ways, the Lord used the Philistines and the Arabs to_____Jehoram. ch: 21

7 - Jeroboam did not become strong again when Abijah was_____; ch: 13

8 - Ahaz gathered the things from God's temple and he_____them into pieces. ch: 28

9 - Many times the glory of the Lord came as a_____at the mountain called Sinai. ch: 6

10 - The Lord called_____, king of Pursia, to make a declaration. ch: 36

12 - The prophets_____Iddo recorded the life of Rehoboam. ch: 12

14 - Jehoshaphat appointed_____in Jerusalem. ch: 19

15 - As the group of priests and Levites came off duty, they did not go home. ch: 23

17 - Jehoshaphat_____in Jerusalem for 25 years. ch: 20

47

Second Chronicles

Across:

29 - As soon as he could,_____brought the leaders of Jerusalem to the temple. ch: 29

31 - Then Solomon went to the towns called Ezion Geber and_____. ch: 8

32 - _____became rich and powerful. ch: 17

34 - Zechariah_____in front of the people and he spoke to them. ch: 24

Down:

21 - Then Zedekiah, son of Chenaanah went to Micaiah and he_____)Micaiah's face. ch: 18

23 - Conaniah and Shemei were_____. ch: 31

25 - Because of his attitude, the people of the 10 tribes refused to accept_____as king. ch: 10

26 - _____came to Asa to show him that his actions were wrong. ch: 16

27 - There was nobody in the royal family to_____Ahaziah. ch: 22

28 - Solomon began to build in his 4th year as_____. ch: 3

30 - So, Hilkiah, and those that the king sent with him, went to talk to_____the Lady prophet. ch: 34

33 - Jotham involved_____in several wars. ch: 27

Second Chronicles

Notes

Ezra

Across:

2 - Also_____Cyrus brought out the objects which belonged to the temple of the Lord. ch: 1

4 - Soon after the people completed the temple, they had the_____holiday. ch: 6

5 - _____recorded the list of people who returned from exile in Babylonia. ch: 2

8 - The Jews who lived during the rule of_____were not a strong nation. ch: 4

10 - The Levites had other musical instruments called_____. ch: 3

11 - The book of Ezra has_____chapters. ch: (kjv)

Down:

1 - Ezra recorded the names of the men who had foreign_____. ch: 10

3 - _____was the chief official in the region beyond the Euphrates river. ch: 5

6 - We left the_____on the 12th day of the first month to go to Jerusalem. ch: 8

7 - Ezra had studied hard and he knew the_____of God. ch: 7

9 - Then at the evening sacrifice, I got up, I had not_____, and I had torn my clothes and my coat. ch: 9

Ezra

Notes

Nehemiah

Across:

4 - They all_____together to come and to fight against Jerusalem. ch: 4

5 - God does_____want his people to worship other gods. ch: 13

7 - Nehemiah recorded this_____of the men who signed the agreement with God. ch: 10

9 - I was the ruler of the country called_____for 12 years. ch: 5

10 - Please hear my prayer and the_____of all your servants. ch: 1

12 - The book of Nehemiah has_____chapters. (kjv)

Down:

1 - Although God looked after his people, they did not_____his law. ch: 9

2 - Ezra opened the book. Everyone could see him because he was_____on the platform above the people. ch: 8

3 - Hanun and the residents of_____repaired the valley gate. ch: 3

4 - _____was the king's agent in all the affairs of the people. ch: 11

6 - _____means to make something clean. ch: 12

8 - It took 52 days to rebuild the_____. ch: 6

10 - But Sanballat, Tobiah and Geshem heard about our_____. ch: 2

11 - These are the people from the towns of Tel Melah, Tel Harsha,_____, Addon, and Immer. ch: 7

Nehemiah

Notes

Esther

Across:

1 - The people that_____wanted to kill were Jews. ch: 3

4 - Only rich and powerful people wore_____clothes. ch: 8

6 - Queen_____had not obeyed her husband. ch: 1

8 - Haman now knows that queen Esther is a_____. ch: 7

9 - Esther could not leave the palace because she was one of the king's_____. ch: 4

10 - Because Mordecai sat at the king's gate, he had_____in the palace. ch: 5

Down:

2 - God had given authority to Easter and_____. ch: 2

3 - The book of Esther has_____chapters. (kjv)

4 - _____is the plural word of "pur" which Haman threw to choose the day to kill the Jews. ch: 9

5 - God is working in the book of Esther. God loves his people and keeps them_____. ch:10

7 - The book of_____contained a report of everything that happened in the kingdom. ch: 6

Esther

Notes

Job

Across:

2 - The enemy in verse 13 is called_____in Hebrew. ch: 26

3 - Joe lacks_____. ch: 34

8 - Job_____God. ch: 23

9 - Job was an_____man. Job was already a true servant of God. ch: 22

11 - In chapter 27 Job was speaking as if he was already in God's_____. ch: 27

13 - God watches_____because he cares about us. ch: 7

14 - God begins to discuss a new subject in these verses. The subject is_____. ch: 38

15 - Job should not accuse_____. ch: 33

17 - A_____approaches. ch: 36

18 - A man_____not accuse God. ch: 40

19 - God is the_____ruler. ch: 25

21 - Job regrets his own_____. ch: 3

25 - The book of Job has forty_____chapters. (kjv)

26 - When Job_____; Job did not respect God. ch: 35

27 - The crocodile_____from the river. ch: 41

28 - _____was sure that God is fair. ch: 8

29 - Job wants to_____. ch: 10

33 - _____was not careful with his words. ch: 5

Down:

1 - Job asked God to take the_____away. ch: 13

4 - In this chapter, Job described many wonderful things. Secrets, Great skills, Beautiful things, and_____. ch: 28

5 - _____was the son of Barakel. ch: 32

6 - A wicked man cannot avoid God's_____. ch: 15

7 - Job_____his friends. ch: 17

8 - So Bildad_____that Job must be a wicked man. ch: 18

10 - God is a fair_____. He will punish a wicked man. ch: 20

12 - Job describes his life before his_____started. ch: 29

14 - Job's_____upset Eliphaz, and Job's troubles also upset Eliphaz. ch: 4

16 - The book of Job teaches us many things about the_____. ch: 1

20 - Job's enemies are like an_____. ch: 30

22 - Job had_____friends. Eliphaz, Bildad, and Zophar. ch: 2

23 - _____cares about Job. ch: 19

24 - Job_____140 years after these events. ch: 42

26 - Perhaps God will punish a wicked man's_____. ch: 21

Job

Across:

35 - Job_____his friends about God. ch; 12

36 - A man cannot_____with God. ch: 9

37 - Job knew that his friends could not help him. His troubles were too_____. ch: 6

40 - God taught a_____about the animals. ch: 39

Down:

30 - I am weak because of my_____. ch: 16

31 - Job's thoughts about a_____that gave him hope. ch: 14

32 - But Job does not know who_____him. ch: 31

34 - _____thought that wicked people always have terrible lives, ch: 11

38 - In_____, evil people will die. ch: 24

39 - The storm sounds like the_____of God. ch: 37

Job

Notes

Psalms 1 – 25

Across:

1 - The Godless do not keep God's rules. God will blow them away like_____one day. #1

8 - _____.His anointed. (The king is speaking). #20

11 - You can see that the_____is incomplete. A few words become changed. #10

13 - _____of the eye. #17

14 - _____of the lip. #22

15 - _____people will one day see the face of God. #11

16 - The_____ words (called verbs) in Psalms 15:2 are different from those in Psalms 15: 3-5. #15

18 - _____sins. These are in contrast to the "errors" or "secret faults" of verse 12. #19

21 - _____. Hebrew word "Nasa" lift up, or "remove" #25

22 - David ask God to be the judge. This means David wants God to give him_____. #7

23 - King David was_____. #6

25 - Be_____. A closing prayer. #21

Down:

2 - There are one_____and fifty numbers of Psalms. (kjv)

3 - That is what "_____your face from me" means. #13

4 - Later David wrote Psalms 8. Perhaps it was when he lived in_____. #8

5 - Lift up your_____. #24

6 - David gives more reasons_____his enemies cannot win. #4

7 - The Lord answered David when he_____. #3

9 - Not_____. Here is the theme of the Psalm. #23

10 - David says that when he became_____, he also became a son of God. #2

12 - _____: The Hebrew word means ropes or cords. #18

17 - David speaks as a prophet. He tells people what God will_____. #12 (verse 5)

18 - David probably wrote Psalm 9 and 10 as one_____. #9

19 - David told the Lord that he would pray early in the_____. #5

20 - _____in Hebrew is the word we get our word Jesus from. #14 (verse 7)

24 - _____Hebrew Azab, literally abandon. #16

Psalms 1 - 25

Notes

Psalms 26 – 50

Across:

2 - _____. Hebrew, means "Ranan" #33

5 - _____. Old English for "Show" #26

6 - "Be_____" Time of silence. #46

7 - "By_____of" Literally, because of the face of, #44

10 - _____. The "Holy of Holies" #28

11 - "_____will go" Hope of joy and praise. #43

13 - Take me_____. From "Asaph" which means, "to gather" #27

14 - _____place. We may not be able to hide physically, but we can rest in Christ. #32

17 - Hand_____. A short length. #39

19 - "_____my case" is from "Rib" which may be translated "contend" #35

20 - In his_____. There was no Holy temple in David's time. #29

22 - _____. Whispering or evil report. #31

23 - _____. From the Hebrew "Cheled" #49

Down:

1 - He_____me. Appreciation and deliverance from fears. #34

3 - _____, or discipline, #50

4 - _____. Rather, "height" #48

6 - _____. David is sing in his heart. #30

8 - _____. Worry not because of evildoers. #37

9 - _____. Infected and putrefying. #38

12 - _____within. When she learned about the planned genocide. #45

14 - _____. The word also means people or gentiles. #47

15 - _____, Hebrew "Tehom" #36

16 - _____down. Literally, bowed down. #42

18 - _____. From "Geber" indicating a man in full vigor. #40

21 - _____. From "Dal" the low, the hopeless, #41

Psalms 26 - 50

Notes

Psalms 51-75

Across:

2 - When I am_____: God is my strength. 56

6 - _____. To "Make Alive" #71

8 - _____. We may grow in Christ to where our loyalty is unmovable. #57

9 - There is a_____. Praise God. #58

10 - _____. We must not neglect this. #55

12 - _____, (consider the context to understand the word). # 52

14 - _____and truth. (The basis of true leadership). #61

15 - _____. Hebrew "Shu'alim" also meaning, "Jackals" #63

16 - But I will_____: (but as for me,) #59

19 - _____. (Those who suffer for his sake). #69

20 - _____. "Damam" meaning to keep quiet. #62

21 - His_____. (Reference to David in verse 1, who represents Christ). #72

23 - We must_____come to him in prayer. #68

24 - _____. (In response to verse 3). #64

Down:

1 - "Let the people praise_____." #67

3 - _____. From "Binedabab" or with "willingness" #54

4 - _____. or ascends. #74

5 - _____: Requests, we may make to the Lord. #51

7 - _____. Turned back. (The Lord had done this in the past). #70

10 - _____. Literally, "Lifting up" #75

11 - _____. Many are called. But few are chosen. #65

13 - _____: A basin for washing. #60

17 - _____: (which is from Yahweh) #53

18 - Heart was_____. (By thinking God was unfair, he was disturbed and prejudiced). #73

22 - _____. Crossing the Jordan. #66

Psalms 51-75

Notes

Psalms 76-100

Across:

1 - _____. Meaning "Mulberry trees" #84

5 - _____. In the poetic parallelism of verse 18. #88

10 - Holy_____. Mount Zion. #99

11 - _____. As if it is the fault of God. #89

15 - _____. Apparently those living south of Idunaea. #83

16 - _____. A stubborn love that will not let us go. #100

18 - _____them or snatch them away. #82

21 - _____. (Thinking and claiming the blessings). #94

22 - _____. "Holy ones" #79

23 - _____. A word used to indicate Egypt. #87

25 - _____out. That is "Prolong" #85

Down:

2 - He_____. (To judge and then take us into heaven). #96

3 - _____. From "Sacred place" #77

4 - _____. They were quails. #78

6 - _____) nations. In the new earth. #86

7 - A_____song. Right hand, (A spectacular deliverance). #98

8 - _____. The three had the same mother. #80

9 - _____. (As when demanding water, as in verse 1). #95

12 - Shalt thou_____: Literally, "You will dress yourself" #76

13 - "_____thee up" (Satan quoted this in tempting Christ). #91

14 - _____of our years. (In contrast to the infinite time of God in verse 9. #90

17 - _____: or "Shout" #81

19 - Clouds and_____. (There are still mysteries beyond our scope of knowing). #97

20 - Clothed..."_____' (The Lord is ready to defend his throne and his word). #93

24 - _____, or "Senseless" #92

Psalms 76-100

Notes

Psalms 101- 125

Across:

3 - _____. Crooked or perverted. #101

5 - _____. From "Taphal" To stick on as a patch. #119

7 - _____. Apparently reference to Sinai. #114

11 - I will_____up mine eyes unto the hills. #121

12 - "At_____" The warning here is against false security. #123

13 - They stand_____forever and ever. #111

14 - "_____the Lord" This is a call for prayer. #105

15 - "The_____of the wicked" It is the scepter or sign of authority. #125

16 - "House of_____" Priests and other spiritual leaders. #115

20 - "_____me" For those who follow the Lord, our troubles may develop our character. #118

21 - "Let his prayer_____sin" Literally, his prayer will become sin. #109

22 - This is the day_____the Lord hath made. #117

23 - "When will I_____" or "Give" #116

Down:

1 - _____. From "Chesed" "Divine love" #107

2 - "_____waters" Flood waters might be proud. #124

4 - _____. His love for us. #103

6 - _____. Thought to be a bush with many twigs called "broom" #120

7 - "_____Glory" (David has dedicated his talents to God). #108

8 - "Until he_____" Literally, until he looks on his enemies. #112

9 - _____. The word is often translated "Cormorant" #102

10 - "_____woman" This is our clue that the Psalm draws from the prayer of Hannah. #113

15 - "Lord at thy_____hand" Christ is at the right hand of the father. #110

17 - _____. That is, "Considered" #106

18 - _____. From "Ruach" which is also translated 'Spirit' #104

19 - For there are_____ thrones of judgments, #122

Psalms 101- 125

Notes

Psalms 126 – 150

Across:

4 - "Hanged our_____" The 144,000 seen standing on MT. Zion. #137

5 - "Not_____" David learned humility. #131

6 - _____. The statement should be obvious to the pagan worshippers. #135

8 - "God of_____" He prevailed. #146

11 - I will praise thee with my_____heart. #138

12 - "_____ Israel" To those of every ethnic background, who call on him. #130

13 - Happy is the man that hath his_____ full of them. #127

15 - _____. Orderly body movements may praise. #149

16 - "_____them" Jesus told us to love our enemies. #139

17 - "It's_____" The Holy Spirit blesses unity where divine love flows through each one of the others. #133

18 - _____. The little plants come up but soon dry out and die. #129

19 - "Lift up_____" A natural attitude of praise. #134

20 - "_____in due season" Is an old word for food. #145

21 - "_____coals" The final destruction of the wicked. #140

22 - _____. (We may expect a harvest of souls). #126

Down:

1 - _____. The Septuagint begins a new Psalm at this point. #147

2 - "To_____" From "Sanach" meaning to sprout. #132

3 - "_____ Children" or Foreign Adversaries. #144

5 - "Make_____" David sounds a little impatient. #141

7 - I remember the days of_____. #143

9 - Let everything that hath_____praise the lord. #150

10 - He hath cut_____the cords of the wicked. #128

11 - "Through the_____" He led and provided. #136

14 - "_____...with my voice" Praying out loud. #142

19 - "_____of his people" Symbols of a beast's power. #148

Psalms 126 - 150

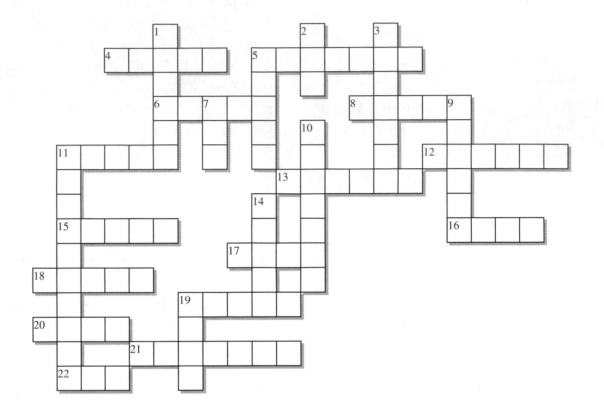

Notes

Proverbs

Across:

5 - _____. Meaning "Squeezing" ch: 30

7 - "_____of my house" Solomon is still speaking to his son: Identify with, void of understanding. ch: 7

8 - _____. Literally, "Stone" ch: 11

9 - Solomon_____the book of Proverbs. ch: 2

11 - _____. Hebrew "Ia'a'"means to talk wildly. ch: 20

14 - _____. The wicked woman is like one with little intelligence. ch: 9

15 - _____is more beautiful than any valuable objects. ch: 3 (verses 23-26).

16 - "That which_____" Them who destroy. ch: 31

17 - The Hebrew word "Maskith" or image, or pictures. ch: 18

19 - The upright choose to live above the wicked world while calling others to follow. ch: 16

20 - _____. From "Nakah" Literally, to fine. ch: 17

24 - "Enemy_____" We are to love our enemies as Jesus does. ch: 24

25 - As in verse 6, the poet compares wisdom to a_____. ch: 4

27 - "_____face" A person is understood in his face. ch: 27

28 - _____. This is like posting bond to keep someone out of jail. ch: 6

29 - _____up a child in the way he should go: ch: 22

Down:

1 - _____. God will expose it in the end. ch: 26

2 - "Slow to_____" Those who take time to understand the reason a person does something. ch: 14

3 - "_____tribute" Staying out of debt is wise. ch: 12

4 - A leaking roof. ch: 19

6 - _____. For the righteous it shines brightly bringing happiness. ch: 13

8 - _____ Means, "Grape juice" ch: 23

10 - "_____thy way" We may pray for protection from temptation, but we must also avoid things that will drag us down. ch: 5

12 - The book of Proverbs has thirty_____chapters. (kjv)

13 - The_____of the wicked shall destroy them. ch: 21

15 - _____. The picture is of aggressively seeking wisdom. ch: 8

18 - _____. Remembering to look at more than the first pointed to. ch: 28

20 - "Way made_____" It is smoothed out. ch: 15

21 - "Cold of_____" Was used by the wealthy to cool drinks. ch: 25

22 - _____. Set on high. ch: 29

23 - Solomon tells us about_____types of persons. ch: 1

26 - "_____lips" He who conceals hatred. ch: 10

Proverbs

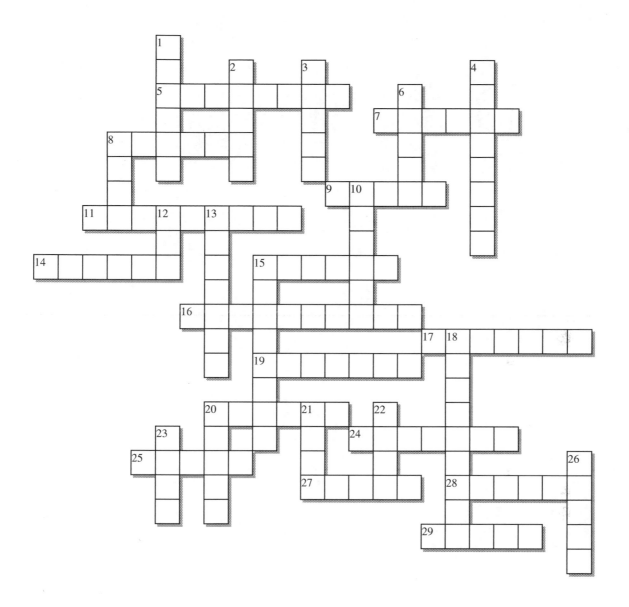

Notes

Ecclesiastes

Across:

2 - _____. Rather, words. ch: 6

5 - _____. That is, acceptable. ch: 10

8 - _____. Think of the aging human body. ch: 12

10 - Give a portion to seven, and also to_____. ch: 11

12 - _____. We should not want to be relieved of trails that shape our character. ch: 7

13 - _____. or cattle. ch: 3

Down:

1 - "_____men" or righteous men. ch: 8

3 - "Gave my_____" Was considered the place of intelligence. ch: 1

4 - _____. From "Besari" my flesh. ch: 2

6 - _____. The Hebrew word is used for a young man. ch: 4

7 - _____. Will the dead live again? Yes. ch: 9

9 - "Love_____" The greedy person is never satisfied. ch: 5

11 - The book of Ecclesiastes has_____chapters. (kjv)

Ecclesiastes

Notes

Song of Solomon

Across:

2 - _____ or Radiant, Solomon here symbolizes the Lord Jesus ch. 5

3 - _____ means Alien ch. 1

5 - _____ from Merkab meaning seat ch. 3

8 - _____ thought to be love apples that encouraged procreation ch. 7

Down:

1 - _____ The name is a feminine form of Solomon ch. 6

4 - _____ on the Lord ch. 8

5 - _____ or 'Secret places of the cliff' ch. 2

6 - The Book of Song of Solomon has _____ Chapters (kjv)

7 - Thou Art _____ the first five verses describe the readiness of Christ's Bride ch. 4

Song of Solomon

Notes

Isaiah

Across:

1 - Fire shall burn _____ the wicked will be completely destroyed at the end of the thousand years ch. 47

2 - _____ or whisper ch. 8

4 - _____They will be dead ch. 66

8 - _____ day when God comes to redeem his waiting ones ch. 26

10 - _____At the coming of Christ ch. 24

13 - _____Hebrew Sheol or Grave ch. 14

14 - _____ city human protection will not avail ch. 27

16 - _____Moab was in troubled waters, unable to swim ch. 25

20 - Indignation cease _____ from God ch. 10

21 - _____It is a call to tell others about our Lord ch. 12

23 - _____As when the Israelites left Egypt ch. 52

25 - Face like a _____Christ had determined from the foundations of the world, To pay the penalty for sin ch. 50

26 - _____Probably near the South end of the Dead Sea ch. 15

29 - _____That is Edom, the land of Esau ch. 34

31 - _____No more invading armies ch. 33

Down:

1 - _____Literally, a place of abomination ch. 30

3 - _____your cause this challenge is for the wicked who are judged ch. 41

5 - Make an _____ agreement. A deception ch. 36

6 - _____A piece of a plant to place in the soli grow ch. 17

7 - _____ or wick reference is to the army of Pharaoh which died in the red sea ch. 43

9 - _____ we do not understand all of the work of God for us ch. 45

11 - _____ from the smoke ch. 9

12 - _____ the heavens Isaiah is looking forward to the day of the Lord's anger ch. 64

15 - _____ A tribe and country of the Ishmaelites in Arabia ch. 21

17 - _____Hebrew 'Meni' translated as 'Destiny' ch. 65

18 - _____He protects and defends those who trust him ch. 31

19 - _____ or zeal or fury ch. 42

21 - _____ of Moab, the Sin of Arrogance ch. 16

22 - _____God's anger is not hatred but seriousness ch. 28

Isaiah

Across:

34 - _____British word for a stag or male deer ch. 35

36 - _____Ancients thought of the sky as a dome. God is above the sky ch. 40

38 - _____ of David, our way of salvation ch. 55

40 - Lift ye up a _____ a signal for destruction ch. 13

42 - _____ or graves, Death as a sleep ch. 57

44 - _____ himself while Christ provides the robe, we have a part ch. 61

45 - Trust in _____ high wickedness will prevail before the coming of Christ. All the power will not bring peace ch. 59

48 - _____ the people would be taken captive ch. 6

49 - _____Solemn message ch.19

51 - _____Apparently flattered ch. 39

53 - Wicked _____ hoping to escape the wrath of God ch. 60

Isaiah

Down:

24 - The Book of Isaiah has _____ six chapters (kjv)

27 - Thou hast _____ our responsibility is to reflect the light that we have been given ch. 48

28 - Their roaring shall be like a _____ ch. 5

30 - _____ God is not at the mercy of those who hate him ch. 1

32 - _____ words, Isaiah was to remember that the messages was not his own ch. 51

33 - _____ the prophecy here is about the King of whom David was a symbol ch. 11

35 - _____ Day, The day of judgement on Israel ch. 4

36 - _____ out rather gaze about ch. 29

37 - Beyond the _____ the Euphrates ch.7

39 - _____ rather beauty ch. 3

41 - _____A person who is selfish or harmful or who behaves badly ch. 32

43 - His _____ Isaiah would have fulfilled this prophecy ch. 44

Isaiah

Across:

54 - _____ of the Lord here the nations would flow into the Holy Mountain ch. 2

57 - Therefore will I put my _____ in thy nose ch. 37

59 - _____The evil or deceptive agreements with other nations ch. 23

61 - _____From Hebrew, TSILTSAL meaning whirring ch. 18

62 - _____A dry tree would bear no fruit ch. 56

Down:

46 - _____When separated while in captivity because of unfaithfulness ch. 54

47 - _____A place to party or to worship the stars ch. 22

49 - Heavy _____ Jesus proclaimed freedom ch.58

50 - _____He was the supposed son of Bel and the second greatest god of Babylon ch. 46

52 - _____Spiritual leaders are to be alert to dangers that threaten the people of God ch. 62

55 - Days of _____ Hebrew Olawm translated forever ch. 63

56 - _____ fathers, or foster fathers ch. 49

58 - _____ the sack cloth, a symbol of release from mourning ch.20

60 - _____From Zera spiritual descendants those who accept his offer of salvation ch. 53

61 - _____ me good reason for singing ch. 38

Isaiah

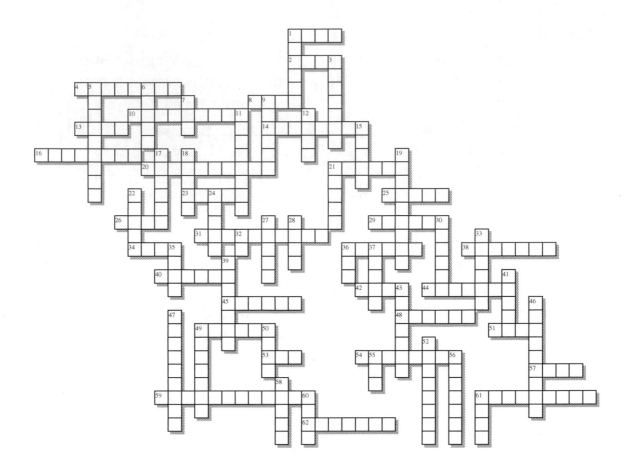

Notes

Jeremiah

Across:

5 - _____From Shama meaning to hear ch. 11

6 - _____Like being burned at the stake ch. 29

8 - And there were ninety and six _____ on a side ch. 52

13 - _____He echoed the warning of Jeremiah ch. 26

15 - _____Another vision, the Lord had given the prophet a puzzle to think about ch. 24

16 - _____Stubbornness ch. 16

17 - _____The Hebrew word also means contend ch. 22

18 - _____A Moabite god ch. 48

19 - _____From Kin'Ah meaning a pack or a bundle ch. 10

20 - _____The family founder who lived 240 years earlier ch. 35

24 - _____From qertes to pinch, to nip ch. 46

25 - _____May also be translated Gather ch. 8

26 - _____ Roll in the chamber, there were chambers in the King's palace round the court or great hall ch. 36

28 - _____Better translated desert ch. 5

30 - _____As the sea ch. 6

32 - _____Wise or skilled ch. 9

Down:

1 - No man _____it the witnesses were all dead ch. 41

2 - _____ God of Israel, the Lord made His no very clear ch. 21

3 - _____Literally vaulted rooms ch. 37

4 - The fathers shall not look back to their _____ for feebleness of hands ch. 47

6 - _____A small number ch. 44

7 - _____Literally head covering ch. 13

9 - _____Confession of guilt ch. 3

10 - _____God sets up and brings down nations ch. 49

11 - _____From may-aw describing deep feelings ch. 4

12 - _____ of mine anger, Literally for my anger ch. 32

14 - _____That is farmers ch. 31

20 - _____ considered to be the rightful King ch. 28

21 - Lovers _____, hopeless case for Judah ch. 30

22 - _____A long linen bandage for dressing wounds ch. 33

23 - _____From 'Chorbah' a place where people used to live ch. 7

25 - Know _____, deep seated wickedness disregards every appeal and warning ch. 42

Jeremiah

Across:

33 - _____ The chief god of Babylon ch. 51

34 - _____ From the Hebrew Rib as appealing in court ch. 2

35 - Go and _____ ; Literally go and buy ch. 19

37 - _____ Hebrew struck with terror ch. 14

39 - _____ A man of strife and contention who lend and borrow ch. 15

40 - _____ From Korea, from a root; to call ch. 17

41 - _____ up The custom of the countries where they wore long garments ch. 1

44 - _____ From Marah, a dual Hebrew form, thus double rebellion ch. 50

47 - Left the _____ , these could occupy the land keeping others from taking over ch. 39

48 - _____ things even in the eyes of the heathen nations ch. 18

49 - _____ A terrible scene for those who reject the mercy of a living God ch. 25

Down:

27 - _____ A poisonous plant ch. 23

29 - _____ Pillars or obeliusks of the place ch. 43

31 - _____ them, Jeremiah was to warn the Kings ch, 27

32 - _____ or worn-out clotes ch. 38

36 - _____ one From arts meaning to tremble ch. 20

38 - The Book of Jeremiah has _____ two chapters (kjv)

42 - _____ destroyed my vineyard ch. 12

43 - _____ Food ch. 40

45 - _____ Jeremiah's stenographer and companion ch. 45

46 - _____ liberty, the slave masters tended to ignore the limited time Hebrew slaves could be kept ch. 34

Jeremiah

Notes

Lamentations

Across:

3 - The Book of Lamentations has _____ chapters. (kjv)

5 - _____From 'Salla Ch' meaning divine forgiveness ch. 3

6 - _____Ash pits, the city was in ashes. ch. 4

8 - _____Glory ch. 2

10 - _____ or staggered ch. 4

11 - _____Prayer for spiritual as well as political restoration. ch.5

Down:

1 - I am becoming _____, may refer to depression. ch. 1

2 - Is _____is to become impure. ch.1

4 - _____ of Jerusalem, this city is often described as a woman. ch. 2

7 - _____ was Black, literally grew hot they had a fever. ch. 5

9 - _____ of the earth, the dead sleeping in their graves. ch. 3

Lamentations

Notes

Ezekiel

Across:

2 - The Lord had brought down the great tree which meant_____. ch: 31

3 - A man who had_____from Jerusalem came to Ezekiel. ch: 33

5 - The valley of the dry_____. ch: 37

7 - "_____my words" Not just part of them. ch: 3

8 - The temple building had_____rooms. ch: 41

9 - The_____are all the same size. ch: 48

13 - Before the priests approach God in the_____area, they must put on special clothes. ch: 44

16 - _____. The direct gift of prophecy. ch: 1

17 - _____. From "Nabal" Failure in moral quality and not simply a lack of understanding. ch: 13

19 - _____came from the family of Esau. ch: 35

20 - _____. The Cherubim. ch: 10

25 - _____. A gesture similar to what we would expect today. ch: 25

27 - Determine, deliberate wickedness. ch: 24

29 - The alter was in_____of the main temple building. ch: 43

31 - _____. He breaks the arms of the king of Egypt. ch: 30

Down:

1 - _____. From "Sawba'im" meaning, uncertain. ch; 23

4 - _____. or exterminated. ch: 6

6 - _____. From "Bo'arim" related to "Be'ir" which means, beasts. ch; 21

8 - _____. A great commercial city and port. ch: 26

10 - _____. or baggage. ch: 12

11 - _____. The end result of rebellion. ch: 15

12 - _____, or represented. ch: 8

13 - God will bring the_____back to their country. ch: 36

14 - The nation's will see the Lord's_____when he punishes them. ch: 39

15 - _____. A city on the coast, about 25 miles north of Tyre. ch: 28

18 - The_____to the building was from the outer area on the east side. ch; 42

20 - _____. Hath resisted my judgements wickedly. ch: 5

21 - _____. Blood for blood. ch: 9

22 - The Lord describes king_____as a large crocodile. ch: 29

23 - The Israelites during Ezekiel's life refused to obey the_____day rules. ch: 46

Ezekiel

Across:

34 - "High_____" The pagans idols at top of hills. ch: 16

35 - The good_____will take care of them. ch: 34

38 - "_____among them" God gives ample evidence but some choose not to believe. ch: 2

40 - Ezekiel saw_____as it flowed from the temple. ch: 47

41 - These gifts will be grain, oil and_____. ch: 45

44 - "Stand in the_____" No one was found. ch: 22

Down:

24 - "_____tools" The elders may have appeared very pious, but inside they had idols and played with temptation. ch: 14

26 - "Set thy face against_____" ch: 38

28 - _____. This means, right. ch: 18

29 - _____. A fortified location. ch: 4

30 - The man took Ezekiel to the east_____of the temple. ch: 40

32 - I will also take of the highest_____of the high cedar. ch: 17

33 - _____. or sounded an alarm. ch: 19

35 - Tyre's end is like a_____that sinks. ch: 27

36 - _____. They lack protection. ch; 11

37 - The Lord told Ezekiel to_____for the Egyptians. ch: 32

39 - "Have_____" He would not act to hold back the punishment. ch: 7

42 - The book of Ezekiel has forty_____chapters. (kjv)

43 - "_____out" Disobedient ones will not be a part of the new Israel. ch: 20

Ezekiel

Notes

Daniel

Across:

1 - Daniel saw_____more angels. ch: 12

5 - Daniel told_____what the message from God meant. ch: 5 (verses 22-28)

6 - The man came to Daniel, but someone stopped him for_____weeks. ch: 10 (verses 10-14)

8 - Daniel was_____that he had done wrong things to God. ch: 9 (verses 5-14)

10 - The book of Daniel has_____chapters. (kjv)

11 - During the time of the Roman kingdom, Jesus was_____. ch: 2 (verses 44-45)

12 - The_____animal means that there will be a_____kingdom on the earth. ch: 7 (verses 23-27)

Down:

2 - Although Nebuchadnezzar was wicked, he was also_____. ch: 1 (verses 3-5)

3 - Nebuchadnezzar was so angry that his_____went red. ch: 3 (verses 19-23)

4 - Nebuchadnezzar told Daniel to_____. ch: 4 (verses 10-12)

7 - The little_____became very proud. ch: 8 (verses 8-12)

8 - "King of the_____" The first to assume this role was Ptolemy. ch: 11

9 - Daniel did not pray in_____. ch: 6 (verses 10-15)

Daniel

Notes

Hosea

Across:

1 - "_____of wine" or raisin cakes. Physical gratification love more than God. ch: 3

2 - Hosea uses the_____of a bird in a good way. ch: 11

3 - "_____me Ishi" The word means my husband. ch: 2

4 - _____. The dominant tribe of the northern kingdom. ch: 7

6 - _____. Literally, stubborn or rebellions. ch: 4

9 - God makes_____to Israel. ch: 14

11 - _____. or chopped up. ch: 6

Down:

1 - The book of Hosea has_____chapters. (kjv)

3 - Hosea says that Israel is worst than_____. ch: 12

5 - Everything in the book of Hosea is a_____from God. ch: 1

6 - "_____for their souls" They would eat what should be brought in offerings. ch: 9

7 - _____. The Ram's-horn. Trumpet. ch: 5

8 - God is angry because_____says false things. ch: 13

10 - "_____the wind" This instead of grain for nourishment. ch: 8

12 - "_____vine" The fruit is turned to false worship. ch; 10

Hosea

Notes

Joel

Across:

4 - _____. Literally, with respect to righteousness. ch: 2

6 - The book of Joel has_____chapters. (kjv)

8 - "Sweet_____" Freshly pressed grape juice. ch: 3

10 - _____. From "Gazam" To cut. ch: 1

11 - _____. Merchant people from S. W. Arabia. ch: 3

Down:

1 - "_____ye priests" These offerings were to provide their food but the situation was more serious. ch: 1

2 - "_____ye" From "Shub" Turn back or return. ch: 2

3 - "Weep_____" The space between the alter in the courtyard and the entrance to the temple. ch: 2

5 - _____. The people are as if drunk. ch: 1

7 - _____. "Achar" In the latter part; ch: 2

9 - _____. Wickedness may seem joyful but is finally bitter sorrow. ch: 1

Joel

Notes

Amos

Across:

2 - Amos now uses_____pictures; no escape; no defense; ch: 5

4 - Amos now uses_____in a clever way. ch: 6 (verse 13)

5 - Amos looked after_____. ch: 1

8 - Amos finishes with a_____. ch: 9

10 - The book of Amos has_____chapters.(kjv)

11 - Amos cries out "_____" ch: 7

Down:

1 - Amos now has a_____picture from God. ch: 8

3 - Judah had broken the special_____, which is for God's people. ch: 2

6 - _____. They do not speak with their own authority; God gives them this authority. ch: 3

7 - In the final verses of Amos there is_____. ch: 9

9 - Amos reminds the Israelites about their time in_____. ch: 4

Amos

Notes

Obadiah

Across:
4 - _____. Servant of Yahweh. ch:1

6 - "_____ day" meaning, the day of judgement for Edom. ch: 1

7 - _____. Those who came to take possession of the city after the return from exile. ch: 1

9 - They are as a_____. ch: 1

10 - "_____ as if" Both wicked and righteous are seen as sleeping after they die. ch: 1

Down:
1 - "_____ yourself" Edom follows the pattern of Lucifer. ch: 1

2 - In the Hebrew bible, these verses are_____. ch: 1

3 - _____. The special words that God uses. ch: 1

5 - Obadiah writes about these events, as if they had already_____. ch: 1

8 - The book of Obadiah has_____ chapter. (kjv)

Obadiah

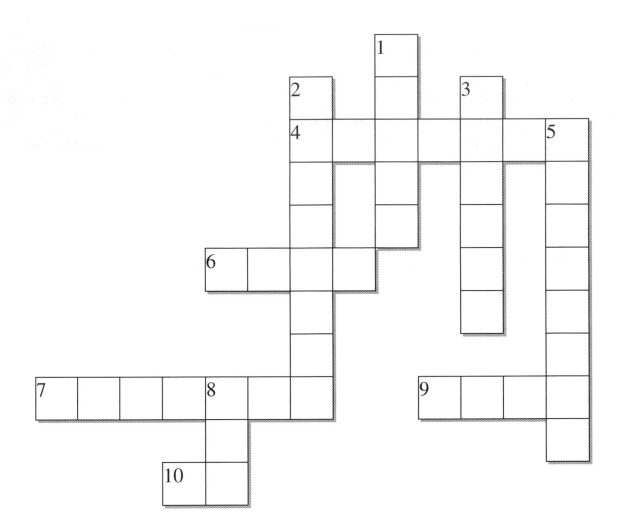

Notes

Jonah

Across:

3 - The book of Jonah has_____chapters. (kjv)

6 - God tells Jonah to go to the great city of_____. ch: 1

8 - "Let me_____" He tells God; ch: 4

9 - The sailors must throw him into the wild_____. ch: 1

10 - The news of Jonah's warning came to the_____of Nineveh. ch: 3

Down:

1 - God heard Jonah's_____for help as he sank into the water. ch: 2

2 - Only God could have_____Jonah. ch: 2

4 - Jonah refused to_____God. ch: 1

5 - Jonah still did not_____, how wrong he was. ch: 4

7 - God wanted Jonah to tell the people to turn from their_____ways. ch: 3

Jonah

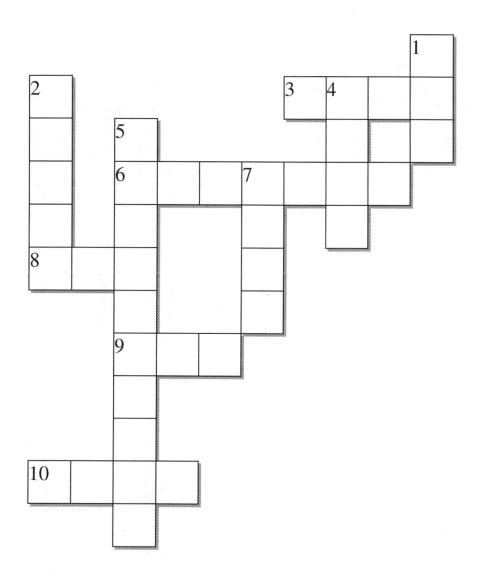

Notes

Micah

Across:

2 - The book of Micah has_____chapters. (kjv)

3 - Micah_____on behalf of God's people. ch; 6

4 - Micah calls together the wicked_____and rulers. ch: 3

7 - They_____poor people in order to become rich. ch: 3

8 - The bible often uses the word_____; It means to be firm. ch: 4

9 - The strong rich people in Israel were_____. ch: 2

Down:

1 - Micah's message is that, the_____will rule the world. ch: 5

4 - Micah had spoken to the people that_____on their beds. ch: 7

5 - Micah gives an order to all the people in_____and Jerusalem. ch: 1

6 - In Micah chapter 4: verse 9, and Micah chapter 5: verse 1, we see the word "_____" four times. ch; 5

Micah

Notes

Nahum

Across:

2 - "Shall_____" From "Nahag" to moan; to lament. ch: 2

5 - Nahum, a town in_____. ch: 1

6 - _____. The Hebrew word is "Shalem" which also means peaceful. ch: 1

7 - The book of Nahum has_____chapters. (kjv)

8 - "_____ways" Nineveh was a large place. ch: 2

9 - _____. The main city of Assyria. ch; 1

11 - _____. spiritual unfaithfulness; ch: 3

Down:

1 - _____. "Taphsarim" table writers or scribes. ch: 3

3 - "Led away_____" or she is laid bare. ch: 2

4 - _____. Molten; standing by the king. ch: 2

8 - "_____city" Assyrians, engraved pictures; killed and tortured freely. ch: 3

10 - _____. The hips and the lower abdomen, regarded as a part of the body to be clothed. ch: 2

Nahum

Notes

Habakkuk

Across:

3 - Habakkuk may have worked with one of the music groups in the temple in_____. ch: 3

6 - _____ will destroy Babylon. ch: 2

8 - Many people are not_____. ch: 2

9 - In chapter 2, it mentions_____things that people do. ch: 2

10 - Habakkuk will be like an animal; this animal is called _____. ch: 3

11 - The prophet is writing about what happens in his own_____. ch: 1

Down:

1 - Many people become_____. ch: 2

2 - The Babylonians have_____gods. ch: 1

4 - The plagues and pestilences are what happened to the_____. ch: 3

5 - There is_____and the law cannot do anything to stop it. ch: 1

7 - The book of Habakkuk has_____chapters. (kjv)

Habakkuk

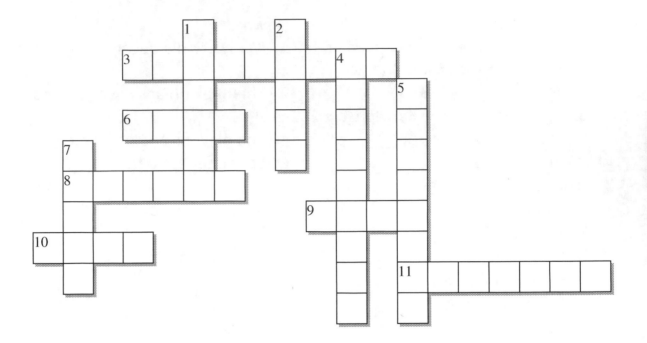

Notes

Zephaniah

Across:

3 - The Lord will_____them afraid, ch: 2

4 - I will bring together_____people among you who want to meet together again. ch: 3

6 - The Lord gave this message to Zephaniah when_____was king. ch: 1

7 - They will build houses but they will never_____in them. ch: 1

8 - When it is time for the Lord's sacrifice, I will_____the rulers and the king's sons. ch: 1

Down:

1 - There money will not_____them. ch: 1

2 - I have_____nations, the Lord says; ch: 3

4 - The book of Zephaniah has_____chapters. (kjv)

5 - That place will become only dry_____. ch: 2

7 - People who pass by the city will make noise with their_____. ch: 2

Zephaniah

Notes

Haggai

Across:

4 - _____. Rain made from ice. ch: 2

5 - God is Lord of_____. ch: 1

7 - _____. It is what a strong wind does to leaves. ch; 2

9 - _____. Something that makes plants ill. ch: 2

Down:

1 - _____said what God told him. ch: 1

2 - _____. A fruit. ch: 2

3 - "_____away" Another picture of inflation. ch: 1

4 - They were not building the_____of God. ch: 1

6 - The book of Haggai has_____chapter. (kjv)

8 - If you put dirty water into clean water, it will all be_____. ch: 2 (verse 13)

9 - "A_____with holes in it" Their money did not buy very much. ch: 1

Haggai

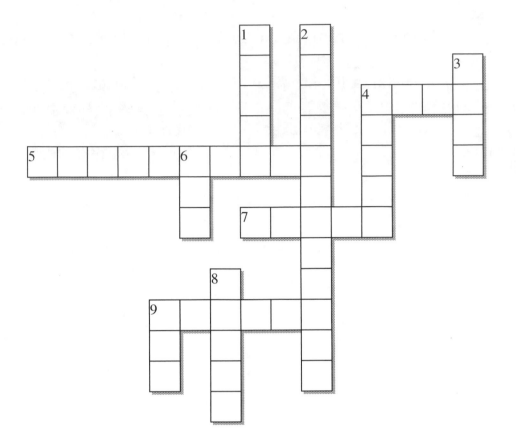

Notes

Zechariah

Across:

2 - _____. The messiah. ch: 3

3 - "_____pieces of silver" The price of a slave and the betrayal price Judas was paid by the priests. ch: 11

5 - _____. In the sanctuary; Lampstand. ch: 4

8 - _____. Whistle; draw the bees by whistling. ch; 10

10 - _____. The need to look to Christ. ch: 6

11 - _____. As the southern extremity of Judah; ch: 14

12 - "The_____that talked with me" The prophet's mentor during the vision. ch: 2

14 - "Repented_____" I did not change my purpose. ch: 8

15 - "Did ye all_____unto me?" It was not divinely appointed. ch: 7

Down:

1 - The myrtle bushes were in a_____. ch: 1

4 - _____. A combination of two Syrian towns. ch: 12

6 - "_____the shepherd" A prophecy about Jesus; ch: 13

7 - _____. A city; state; N. E. of Syria. ch: 9

9 - The book of Zechariah has_____chapter. (kjv)

13 - _____. A unit of dry measure equivalent to about 5 gallons. ch: 5

Zechariah

Notes

Malachi

Across:

1 - The animals were unholy to_____to God. ch: 2

4 - _____will not fall off the vines until they are ripe. ch: 3

5 - When you offer the Lord these_____things, he will not accept your gifts. ch: 1

7 - _____. Hebrew; "Torah" ch: 4

8 - God speaks about_____as if he is one man. ch; 2

9 - _____. A yard around the building. ch: 2

10 - _____. Means, Sinai. ch: 4

Down:

2 - The book of Malachi has_____chapters. (kjv)

3 - "The_____of Jacob" means, all the Jews. ch: 3

4 - _____. Kinder, than you need to be. ch: 2

6 - The people did not agree that God_____them. ch: 1

9 - God_____not to love Esau. ch: 1

Malachi

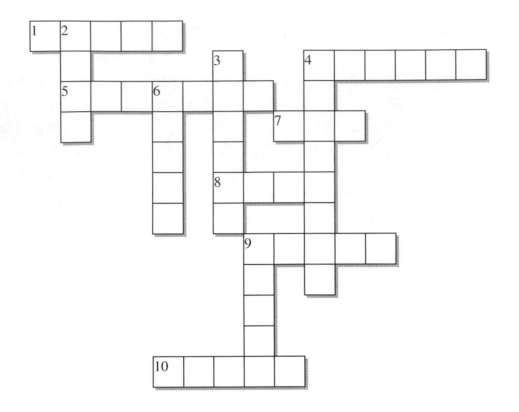

Notes

Matthew

Across:

3 - "_____them" was to be accompanied by teaching; ch: 28

5 - Jesus reminded the_____man about five of God's ten commandments. ch: 19

6 - "_____is weak" What can we do about weak: ch: 26

7 - Jesus stated "The last people will be first, and the_____people will be last" ch: 20

8 - Jesus was_____. ch: 3

11 - The book of St. Matthew has twenty_____ chapters. (kjv)

13 - Jesus says that_____will come to families. ch: 10

16 - The hidden treasure and the_____that had great value. ch: 13

18 - Jesus speaks about his_____. ch: 16

20 - O _____, our Lord's heart cry for his people. ch: 23

22 - St. Matthew does not tell us the name of the_____. ch: 17

24 - People with all kinds of_____came to get help. ch: 4

25 - Christ is a _____word, and the same word in the Hebrew language is messiah. ch: 1

26 - Jesus used the words "_____of man" to describe himself. ch: 8

Down:

1 - The Pharisees and teachers ask Jesus for a_____. ch: 12

2 - The most important of God's commandment is that people should love_____. ch: 22

3 - _____, means "House of Bread" ch:2

4 - _____. An area on the north west side of the lake. ch: 14

9 - Jesus_____ 4,000 people. ch: 15

10 - The_____people were very proud. ch: 11

12 - A wise man makes sure he builds his_____in a strong place. ch: 7

13 - _____or three people who pray together have Jesus with them. ch: 18

14 - "As the_____" the coming of Christ will be visible; ch: 24

15 - St. Matthews story showed that the_____had failed, so it was the right time to destroy it. ch: 21

17 - The_____were proud of themselves because they obeyed the law. ch: 5

18 - People often refer to such an evil spirit as a_____. ch: 9

19 - "Ten_____" Unmarried young women who represent people with the light of truth. ch: 25

21 - "_____God, my God; ch: 27

23 - The Jews prayed_____times in one day. ch: 6

Matthew

Notes

Mark

Across:

2 - Jesus becomes_____again. ch: 16

5 - No one knows the day or the_____when all these things will happen. ch: 13

6 - The soldiers put Jesus on a_____. ch: 15

8 - Jesus stops a_____. ch: 4

9 - St. Mark wrote this book while living in_____. ch: 1

10 - Herod_____ruled Galilee from 4 BC to 39 AD. ch: 6

13 - Jesus chooses_____Apostles. ch: 3

15 - It is easier for a camel to go through the eye of a_____; ch: 10

Down:

1 - _____. Do not believe that anyone can become alive again after death. ch: 12

3 - A person could say, to this mountain "_____and throw yourself into the sea" ch: 11

4 - Small pieces of_____drop while the children eat. ch: 7

6 - If your hand causes you to do wrong things, you should_____it off. ch: 9

7 - Who do_____say that I am? ch: 8

8 - She said if I may touch but his clothes, I_____be whole. ch: 5

11 - The book of St. Mark has_____chapters. (kjv)

12 - A woman pours expensive oil on Jesus'_____. ch: 14

14 - Jesus helps a man who cannot_____. ch: 2

Mark

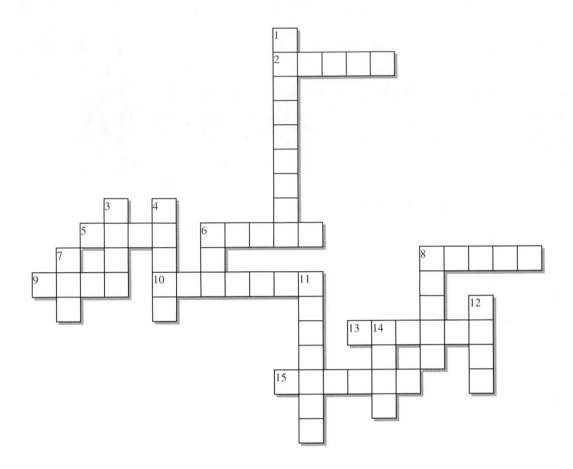

Notes

Luke

Across:
2 - The_____of faith. ch: 17
4 - John_____Jesus. ch: 3
5 - Jesus explains why he uses_____.
ch: 8
7 - Mary and Joseph returned to
their own town of_____. ch: 2
9 - The_____. ch: 24
11 - Jesus_____ 5000 people. ch: 9
12 - A message to_____about the
birth of Jesus. ch: 1
13 - A Pharisee_____Jesus to have
dinner with him. ch: 7
14 - The_____young ruler. ch: 18
16 - The book of ST. Luke
has_____four chapters. (kjv)
19 - The rich man and_____. ch: 16
20 - The death of_____. ch: 23
22 - The widow's_____. ch: 21
23 - Jesus cures a man with_____.
ch: 5
24 - Jesus heals a man on the_____.
ch: 14

Down:
1 - Paying taxes to_____. ch: 20
2 - Making_____with God. ch: 12
3 - The_____of disciples. ch: 6
6 - Jesus was in the_____forty days.
ch: 4
8 - Jesus teaches about_____. ch: 11
10 - The parable of the good_____.
ch: 10
15 - The parable of the_____son. ch:
15
17 - The parable of the_____. ch: 13
18 - Jesus and_____. ch: 19
21 - The Lord's_____. ch: 22

Luke

Notes

John

Across:

2 - "Find no_____" Condemnation for the accusers. ch: 18

4 - _____. Christ does through the bible. ch: 17

5 - _____. Literally, A pretext. ch: 15

9 - The_____was the most important Jewish festival. ch: 2

10 - "Hath_____life" As Christ has taken our flesh we may receive his spiritual life. ch: 6

12 - Jesus_____an official's son. ch: 4

13 - "I am_____" The word; He, is supplied as it is in the Septuagint. ch: 8

16 - "Did not_____" Literally, continued to not acknowledge. ch: 12

17 - "Give up the_____" meaning, his breath; he laid down his life. ch: 19

18 - The book of St. John has twenty_____chapters. (kjv)

19 - _____. "My great one" ch: 20

20 - "Jesus_____" "Dakrud" meaning crying of tears. ch: 11

Down:

1 - "Of_____" The Holy Spirit reveals a portion of the truth from Christ. ch: 16

3 - _____. Greek "Agapos" Love based on principle. ch: 21

5 - _____. Without any evidence of wrong doing, followers of Christ would be hated and punished. ch: 7

6 - John the Baptist was a_____. ch: 1

7 - John the Baptist and Jesus' disciples' were_____people. ch: 3

8 - _____. Compared "Lamp" to the True Light, which is Christ. ch: 5

11 - "_____the Jordan" He stayed in Persia for some time. ch: 10

12 - "The_____" Greek word "Parakletos" meaning one called to one's side. ch: 14

14 - "Since the word_____" Literally, "from the age" ch: 9

15 - _____, or Morsel, or Piece. ch: 13

John

Notes

\

Acts

Across:

2 - It was done with a_____; on the end of a rope; how far down it was to the bottom. ch: 27

3 - _____. False doctrine would come into the church. ch: 20

5 - _____. Annoyed and aroused. ch: 4

6 - _____. Literally, who is called. ch: 15

8 - "_____and Hebrews" Those who came from Greek countries. ch: 6

10 - _____. An invitation to accept salvation in Christ. ch: 2

11 - _____. or Prophesying. ch: 16

12 - _____. A word imitating a language not understood. ch: 28

14 - _____, or Phonecia; The area of Tyre and Sidon. ch: 11

17 - _____. Seaport for Corinth; east of the city. ch: 18

18 - _____. A seaport. ch: 9

19 - _____. The gift of the spirit. ch: 10

20 - _____. Fault or impropriety. ch: 25

22 - _____. A respected Teacher, grandson of famous Hillel and a Pharisee. ch: 5

25 - _____. The seat of the Roman government in Palestine. ch: 23

26 - _____, or Reasoning. ch: 19

27 - _____. Greek "Anakrino" A mindless penalty. ch: 12

Down:

1 - _____. From "Sebasmata" Objects of worship. ch: 17

4 - _____. He prophesied a famine. ch: 21

7 - _____. "The Potter's Field" ch: 1

9 - "People_____" This miracle was a witness to the ministry of the Holy Spirit. ch: 3

11 - _____. Refers to the province; the chief city. ch: 8

13 - _____. or signaling. ch: 13

14 - _____. Coastal area. ch: 14

15 - _____. or Gentleness. ch: 24

16 - _____. Later the apostle Paul who was sent to the gentiles. ch: 7

21 - _____. From "Martus" meaning witness. ch: 22

23 - _____. The light wasn't sunshine. ch: 26

24 - The book of Acts has twenty_____chapters. (kjv)

Acts

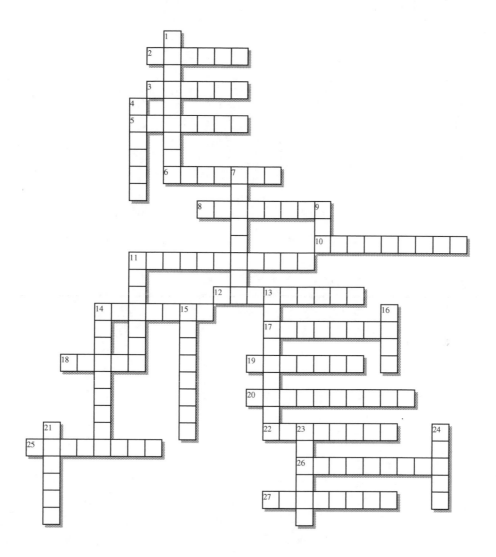

Notes

Romans

Across:

2 - _____. It means "passing over" rather than forgiveness. ch: 3

4 - _____. The area of Dalmatia and north (what is now Croatia). ch: 15

7 - _____. "Slave" Greek "Doulos" Paul recognized that Christians are voluntary slaves to Christ. ch: 1

8 - _____. The name means brilliant or bright. ch: 16

13 - Free grace. ch: 11

14 - _____. From "Koinoeno" To share; or to take part in. ch: 12

15 - _____. Emotions or Passions. ch: 7

16 - _____. Truth and salvation are not based on how many people believe a popular way. ch: 9

17 - _____. or argues with himself. ch: 14

Down:

1 - "_____not" Paul is describing a principle; he is not opposed to work. ch: 4

3 - _____. From "Leitourgoi" servants or public servants. ch: 13

5 - "_____not sin" You won't allow sin to be your master. ch: 6

6 - "Doers of the_____" It is the standard of righteousness. ch: 2

9 - "_____of the law" Goals; It is fulfilled in Christ. ch: 10

10 - _____. From "Proginosko" to know ahead of time. ch: 8

11 - The book of Romans has_____chapters. (kjv)

12 - "In_____time" At the right time. ch: 5

Romans

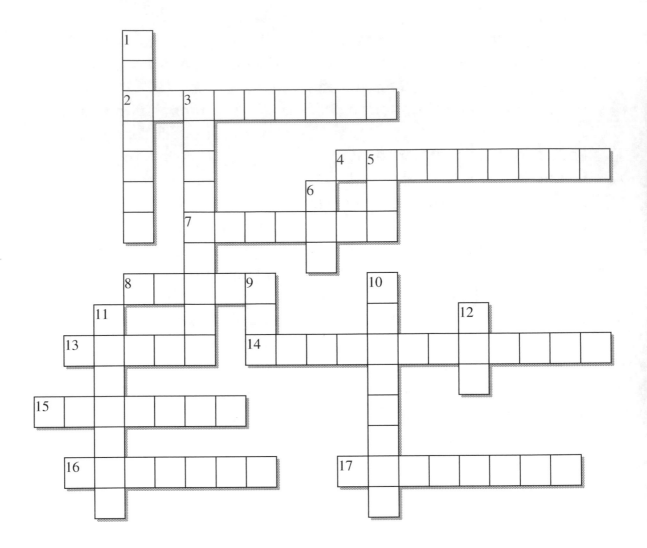

Notes

First Corinthians

Across:

3 - _____. That is, anxious care. ch: 7

5 - _____. "O Lord come" ch: 16

6 - "_____of God" We are responsible to preserve our bodies and souls both spiritually and physically. ch: 3

7 - _____. Greek "Makellon" Meat market. ch: 10

10 - _____, or admonish. ch: 4

11 - _____. Senseless one. ch: 15

12 - _____. A responsibility. ch: 6

13 - _____. From "Didache" Teaching. ch: 14

16 - _____. People with different ideas and different opinions. ch: 11

Down:

1 - _____. Greek "Adokimos" unapproved. ch: 9

2 - "_____out" Contamination was to be avoided. The person was to be put out of the church. ch: 5

4 - _____. From "Oikodomeo" to build up. ch: 8

7 - "_____long" or is patient. ch: 13

8 - The book of 1st Corinthians has_____chapters. (kjv)

9 - _____. From "Pis'tis" moral conviction. ch: 12

14 - _____. "Peter" Transliterated from Aramaic "Kepha" ch: 1

15 - _____. From "Anakrino" to investigate. ch: 2

First Corinthians

Notes

Second Corinthians

Across:

1 - _____. or test. ch: 8

3 - _____. The Southern part of Greece, Macedonia was the Northern part. ch: 1

4 - _____. Paul was afraid many would lose their spirituality. ch: 12

7 - We must all appear before the_____seat of Christ. ch: 5

8 - _____. From "Adokimoi" test failers. ch: 13

10 - _____. Providing seed; spiritual seed. ch: 9

12 - Be ye not unequally_____together with unbelievers. ch: 6

13 - _____. From "Hauchaomai" This word is used 32 times in this epistle. ch: 10

Down:

1 - The book of 2nd Corinthians has_____chapters. (kjv)

2 - _____. Where the spirit of the Lord is. ch: 3

5 - _____. The discipline administered by the church was enough. ch: 2

6 - Empathy is encouraged. ch: 11

9 - _____. or sad. ch: 7

11 - The_____man is renewed day by day. ch: 4

Second Corinthians

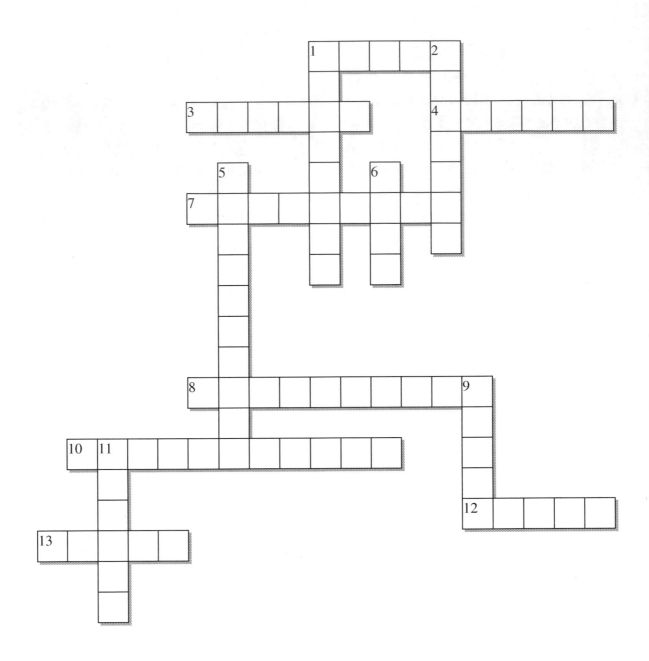

Notes

Galatians

Across:

3 - _____. From "Anastrophe" meaning behavior or conduct. ch: 1

5 - _____. or credited. ch; 3

6 - The book of Galatians has_____chapters. (kjv)

7 - _____. or in order to purchase the freedom. ch: 4

Down:

1 - _____. Sets the feeling. ch: 5

2 - And let us not be_____in well doing. ch; 6

4 - _____. Denying the power of Christ. ch: 2

Galatians

Notes

Ephesians

Across:
2 - "_____my knees" humility, in prayer. ch: 3

3 - Literally, having been alienated. ch: 2

5 - "_____husband" It is to emphasize the marriage responsibility. ch: 5

6 - _____. Those who are following Christ; the direction of the final development. ch: 4

Down:
1 - _____. Greek "Ouranos" meaning everywhere. ch: 1

2 - _____. or all the congregation. ch: 6

4 - The book of Ephesians has_____chapters. ch: (kjv)

Ephesians

Notes

Philippians

Across:

4 - The book of Philippians has_____chapters. (kjv)

5 - _____. From "Autarkes" Sufficient for oneself. ch: 4

7 - _____. Yielding or kindness. ch: 4

8 - _____. From "Akeraioi" cannot be accused. ch: 2

9 - I count not myself to have_____; ch: 3

Down:

1 - _____. or falsely alleged motive. ch: 1

2 - Beware of_____. Beware of evil workers. ch: 3

3 - _____. Greek "Koinonia" partnership. ch: 2

6 - For me to live is Christ, and to die is_____. ch: 2

Philippians

Notes

Colossians

Across:

2 - Paul used_____in his language. ch: 2

5 - _____not one to another. ch; 3

7 - Paul sent_____men to Colossians with this letter. ch: 4

8 - And increasing in the_____of God. ch: 1

10 - _____was in prison when he wrote this letter. ch: 1

Down:

1 - The book of Colossians has_____chapters. (kjv)

3 - _____are responsible for the way they behave towards other people. ch; 3

4 - Yet am I with you in the_____. ch: 2

6 - That he hath a great_____for you. ch: 4

9 - _____be with you. ch: 4

Colossians

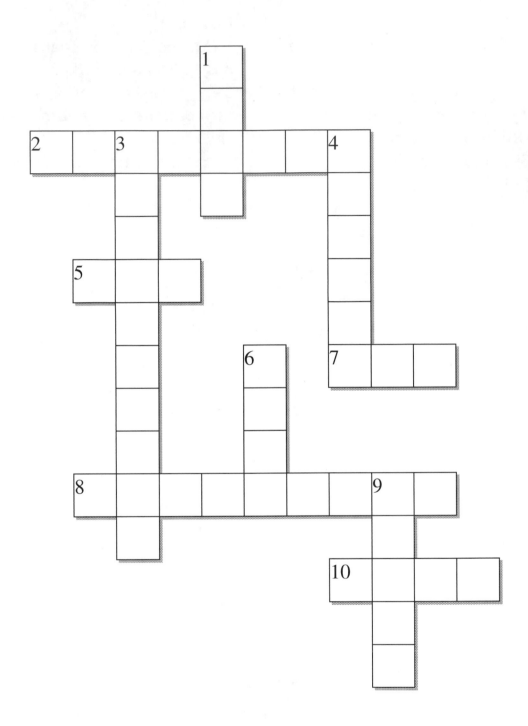

Notes

First Thessalonians

Across:

2 - Greetings from Paul, _____and Timothy. ch: 1

4 - _____ or in much conflict. ch: 2

7 - _____. Greek "Porneia" Aphrodite was goddess of love and generation. ch: 4

9 - _____. From all appearance of evil. ch: 5

10 - The book of 1st Thessalonians has_____chapters. (kjv)

Down:

1 - If ye stand_____in the Lord. ch: 3

3 - Paul and his friends spoke about the_____news of Jesus. ch: 1

5 - _____. From "Paraklesis" comfort; ch: 2

6 - _____. Greek "Nephomen" meaning, without wine. ch: 5

8 - _____. Silas and Timothy remained in Macedonia when Paul had to leave. ch: 3

9 - _____. They are described as sleeping. ch: 4

First Thessalonians

Notes

Second Thessalonians

Across:

2 - Which is the_____in every epistle; ch: 3

3 - By the_____of our Lord Jesus Christ. ch; 2

5 - Wherefore_____we pray always for you; ch: 1

8 - _____your hearts; ch: 2

9 - But the Lord is_____; ch: 3

10 - _____fast; ch: 2

Down:

1 - _____. Not in uncontrolled temper but in justice. ch: 1

2 - We are bound to_____God always for you. ch: 1

3 - That our God would count you worthy of this_____. ch; 1

4 - Be not_____in well doing; ch: 3

6 - And for this cause God shall send them strong_____; ch: 2

7 - The book of 2nd Thessalonians has_____chapters. (kjv)

Second Thessalonians

Notes

First Timothy

Across:

2 - _____. Overseer. ch: 3

5 - "Under the_____" Spiritual freedom which led to physical freedom. ch; 6

6 - _____. To put into order. ch: 2

7 - That they be not_____. ch: 6

11 - "_____widows" Helping with their needs as well as with kindness. ch: 5

12 - The book of 1st Timothy has_____chapters. (kjv)

Down:

1 - _____. Being a christian leader is standing by grace against the powers of darkness. ch: 1

2 - _____. Woven, twisted together. ch: 2

3 - _____. Greek "Nephalios" Abstaining from fermented wine. ch: 3

4 - _____. Predictions at the time of Timothy's ordination. ch: 1

8 - _____. From "Meletao" To attend to carefully. ch: 4

9 - _____. Descendants. ch: 5

10 - "_____exercise" We must not neglect exercise. ch: 4

First Timothy

Notes

Second Timothy

Across:

3 - "_____trouble" From "Kapatheo" To suffer evil; ch: 2

5 - _____. From "Apologia" meaning, defence. ch: 4

6 - _____. According to biblical principles. ch: 2

9 - _____. From "Adikia" Unrighteousness. ch: 2

10 - "Great_____" The church. ch: 2

11 - _____. A new attitude. ch: 2

Down:

1 - _____. Maybe; ch: 2

2 - "_____us the spirit" The gift includes a sound mind. ch: 1

4 - _____. From "Anoia" meaning, lack of understanding. ch: 3

6 - "Youthful_____" From"Epithumiai" meaning, desires. ch: 2

7 - "Before the_____began" Before eternal times. ch: 1

8 - The book of 2nd Timothy has_____chapters. (kjv)

Second Timothy

Notes

Titus

Across:

2 - _____. From "Periousios" meaning, chosen. ch: 2

3 - Looking for the blessed_____; ch: 2

5 - _____. Speech. ch: 2

8 - The book of Titus has_____chapters. (kjv)

9 - "_____elders" A plan of church organization. ch: 1

Down:

1 - _____. Happy. ch: 2

2 - _____. Before the world began. ch: 1

4 - But avoid foolish_____; ch: 3

6 - _____. All meekness unto all men; ch: 3

7 - _____. Slave. ch: 1

10 - The_____woman likewise; ch: 2

Titus

Notes

Philemon

Across:

3 - _____. The only record we have about him. ch: 1

4 - _____. or our sister. ch: 1

5 - "I_____" From "Boulomai" meaning, to desire; ch: 1

7 - But without thy_____would I do nothing; ch: 1

8 - _____. A runaway slave. ch: 1

Down:

1 - _____. or useful. ch: 1

2 - Put that on_____account; ch: 1

4 - _____. Feelings or emotions. ch: 1

6 - _____. He has turned back to the world. ch: 1

8 - The book of Philemon has_____chapter. (kjv)

Philemon

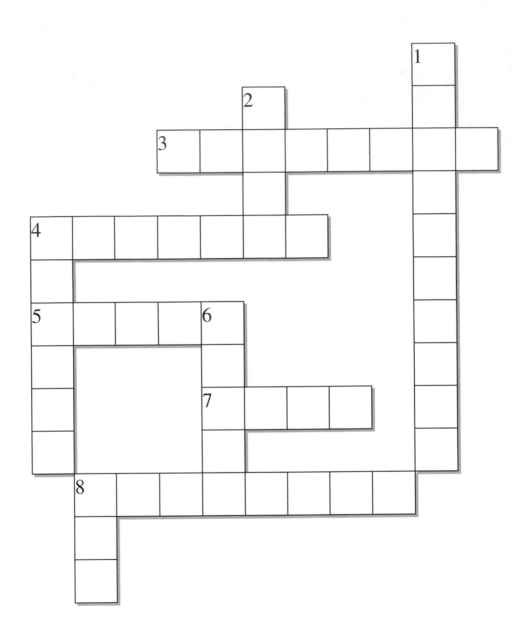

Notes

Hebrews

Across:

2 - _____. or maturity. ch: 6

4 - _____. or greeted. ch: 11

7 - _____. or innocent. ch: 7

11 - "By_____of use" Habit. ch: 5

12 - I will put my trust in_____. ch: 2

13 - _____. Those who died in the wilderness. ch: 4

14 - Be not carried about with_____and strange doctrine; ch: 13

Down:

1 - _____. Jesus Christ was commissioned to be our savior. ch: 1

3 - Not_____the assembling of ourselves together; ch: 10

5 - _____. From "Egkainizo" meaning, inaugurate. ch: 9

6 - The book of Hebrews has_____chapters. (kjv)

8 - Wherefore_____up the hands which hang down; ch: 12

9 - "The_____" From "Hagia" meaning, The Holies; ch: 8

10 - _____. Not with hatred; ch: 3

Hebrews

Notes

James

Across:

2 - _____. Comfortable with own ideas. ch: 1

4 - _____. When we hurt others, we confess to them. ch: 5

6 - _____. From"Machai" meaning, individual arguments. ch: 4

8 - "Tame the_____" A wild tongue. ch: 3

9 - And I will shew thee my faith by_____works; ch: 2

10 - _____. Do the word. ch: 1

Down:

1 - _____. From "Polemoi" meaning, quarrels. ch: 4

2 - The_____waiteth for the precious fruit of the earth; ch: 5

3 - And are become_____of evil thoughts? ch: 2

5 - The book of James has_____chapters. (kjv)

7 - _____. From "Eritheia" meaning, working to strengthen a group against others. ch: 3

James

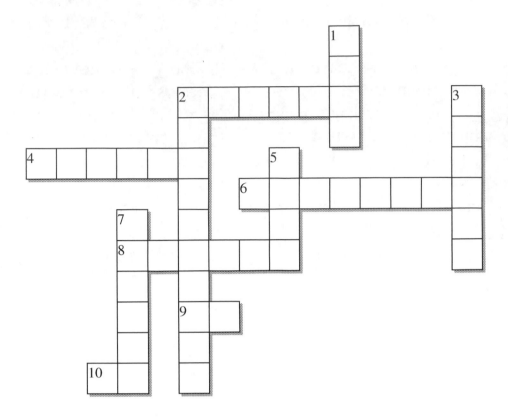

Notes

First Peter

Across:

4 - _____. God made us. ch; 4

6 - The book of 1st Peter has_____chapters. (kjv)

9 - Desire the sincere_____of the word. ch: 2

10 - _____. Humility towards God. ch: 3

Down:

1 - Wherefore_____up the loins of your mind. ch: 1

2 - A royal_____; ch: 2

3 - _____. From "Anupokritos" meaning, undisguised. ch: 1

5 - _____. From "Ptoesis" meaning, fear. ch: 3

7 - _____. Therefore; ch: 4

8 - _____. According to God's will. ch: 5

11 - _____. From "Anthistemi" meaning, to withstand. ch: 5

First Peter

Notes

Second Peter

Across:

2 - For he received from God the father_____and glory; ch: 1

4 - The book of 2nd Peter has_____chapters. (kjv)

6 - Add to your faith_____; ch: 1

8 - And a thousand years as_____day. ch: 3

9 - They_____through the lusts of the flesh; ch: 2

10 - "Gone_____" Having been caused to wander. ch: 2

Down:

1 - The dog is turned to his own_____again. ch: 2

3 - _____. Greek "Luo" meaning, to loosen. ch: 3

5 - And cannot_____afar off. ch: 1

7 - "Willingly_____" A choice to doubt. ch: 3

Second Peter

Notes

First John

Across:

3 - For sin is the_____of the law. ch: 3

6 - He that believeth not God hath made him a_____; ch: 5

7 - But_____love casteth out fear; ch: 4

11 - But try the_____whether they are of God. ch: 4

12 - And_____one another; ch: 3

Down:

1 - And he is the_____for our sins; ch: 2

2 - Let no man_____you; ch: 3

4 - And_____his brother. ch: 3

5 - But ye have an_____from the holy one; ch: 2

8 - The book of 1st John has_____chapters. (kjv)

9 - Which_____is true in him and in you; ch: 2

10 - That your_____may be full; ch: 1

11 - Now are we the_____of God; ch: 3

First John

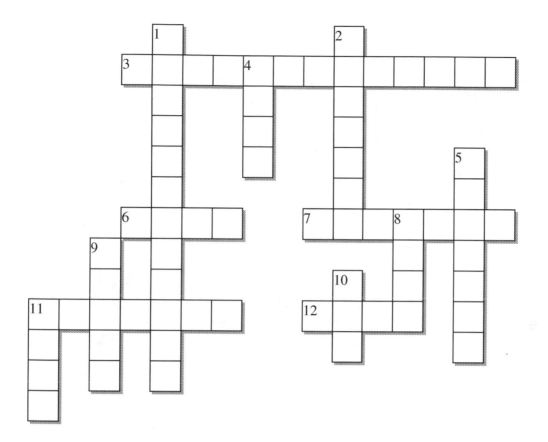

Notes

Second John

Across:
3 - And_____face to face; ch: 1
5 - Look to_____; ch: 1
7 - And now I_____thee. ch: 1
8 - Whom I love in the_____; ch: 1
10 - And_____I only. ch: 1

Down:
1 - _____be with you; ch: 1
2 - And this_____love; ch: 1
4 - But that we receive a full_____;
ch: 1
6 - The book of 2nd John
has_____chapter. (kjv)
9 - _____not God. ch: 1

Second John

Notes

Third John

Across:
1 - And to_____; ch: 1
5 - If I_____; ch: 1
7 - I will not with_____and pen write unto thee; ch: 1
8 - Thou_____do well; ch: 1
10 - _____be to thee; ch: 1

Down:
2 - Greet the friends by_____. ch: 1
3 - For I_____greatly; ch: 1
4 - _____not that which is evil; ch: 1
6 - I wrote unto the_____; ch: 1
9 - The book of 3rd John has_____chapter. (kjv)

Third John

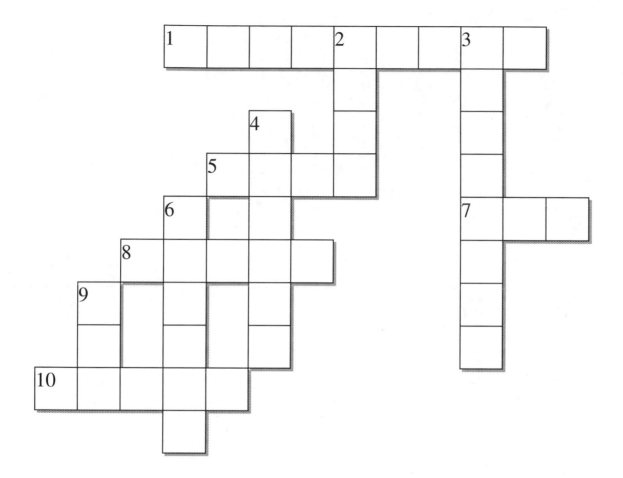

Notes

Jude

Across:

1 - Be glory and_____; ch: 1

3 - And_____of James; ch: 1

4 - I will therefore put you in_____; ch: 1

7 - Trees whose_____withereth; ch: 1

9 - Making a_____; ch: 1

10 - Walking after their own_____; ch: 1

Down:

1 - These are_____; ch: 1

2 - Yet_____the arch angel; ch: 1

5 - As_____beasts; ch: 1

6 - It was_____for me to write unto you; ch: 1

8 - The book of Jude has_____chapter. (kjv)

Jude

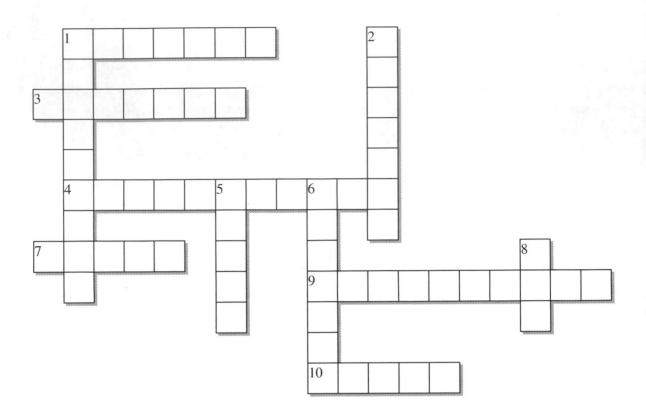

Notes

Revelation

Across:

4 - _____. John was there as a Roman prisoner. ch: 1

5 - John_____seven angels. ch: 15

7 - An Elder spoke to John and asked him_____questions; ch: 7

9 - _____. Those who doubt try to close the door for others. ch: 3

12 - The_____seals. ch: 6

13 - Then every person who had died stood in front of the_____. ch: 21

14 - John saw a great_____dragon. ch: 12

16 - The 7th trumpet sounded; John was in_____. ch: 11

19 - _____. In place of father; ch: 2

20 - "_____hand" Representing his power to act; ch: 5

21 - The seven bowls of God's_____. ch: 16

Down:

1 - The_____of the woman were purple and bright red. ch: 17

2 - Then I saw another beast which came out of the_____. ch: 13

3 - The strong angel and the little_____. ch: 10

5 - Jesus says, watch carefully; I am coming_____. ch: 22

6 - Heaven opens and I saw a_____horse. ch: 19

7 - The book of Revelation has_____two chapters. (kjv)

8 - Messages from the_____angels. ch: 14

10 - The seven_____. ch: 8

11 - And_____I was in the spirit; ch: 4

15 - Christ had ruled the earth for 1000_____. ch: 20

17 - The funeral of_____. ch: 18

18 - John saw a_____, it had just fallen from the sky. ch: 9

Revelation

Notes

References

Bryant, T. Alton, <u>Zondervan's Compact Bible Dictionary</u>, June 1, 2001

Baker Publishing Group, New Combined Bible Dictionary and Concordance (Direction Bks), June 1, 1973

Godwin, Johnnie, Phyllis Godwin & Karen Dockery, The Student Bible Dictionary Jan 1, 2001

Merriam-Webster Dictionary, copyright 2011.

Spence, H.D.M & Joseph S. Exell. The Pulpit Commentary, 1985.

DR VBS MINISTRIES

"Growth Is A Necessity For Life"

Web site: www.drvbsministries.com